Living in the Presence of the Future

The London Lectures in Contemporary Christianity

This is an annual series of lectures founded in 1974 to promote Christian thought about contemporary issues. Their aim is to expound an aspect of historical biblical Christianity and to relate it to a contemporary issue in the church in the world. They seek to be scholarly in content yet popular enough in appeal and style to attract the educated public; and to present each topic in such a way as to be of interest to the widest possible audience as well as to the Christian public.

Recent lectures:

1994 'Transforming Leadership: A Christian approach to managing organizations', *Richard Higginson*

1995 'The Spirit of the Age', *Roy McCloughry* (published by IVP in 2001 as *Living in the Presence of the Future*)

1996 'The Word on the Box': Christians in the media', *Justin Phillips, Graham Mytton, Alan Rogers, Robert McLeish, Tim Dean*

1997 'Matters of Life and Death': Contemporary medical dilemmas in the light of the Christian faith', *Professor John Wyatt* (published by IVP in 1998 as *Matters of Life and Death: Today's healthcare dilemmas in the light of Christian faith*)

1998 'Endless Conflict or Empty Tolerance: The Christian response to a multi-faith world', *Dr Vinoth Ramachandra* (published by IVP in 1999 as *Faiths in Conflict: Christian integrity in a multicultural world*)

2000 'The Incomparable Christ: Celebrating his millennial life', *John Stott*

The London Lectures Trust

The London Lectures in Contemporary Christianity are organized by the London Lectures Trust, which was established as a charity in 1994. The committee represents several different evangelical organizations.

Living in the Presence of the Future

Roy McCloughry

December 2000
Based on the London Lectures
in Contemporary Christianity

ivp
Inter-Varsity Press

INTER-VARSITY PRESS
38 De Montfort Street, Leicester LE1 7GP, England
Email: ivp@uccf.org.uk
Website: www.ivpbooks.com

© Roy McCloughry 2001

Roy McCloughry has asserted his right under the Copyright, Designs and Patents Act, 1988, to be identified as Author of this work.

All rights reserved. No part of this publication may be reproduced, stored in a retrieval system, or transmitted, in any form or by any means, electronic, mechanical, photocopying, recording or otherwise, without the prior permission of the publisher or the Copyright Licensing Agency.

Unless otherwise stated, Scripture quotations in this publication are from the Holy Bible, New International Version. Copyright ©1973, 1978, 1984 by International Bible Society. Used by permission of Hodder & Stoughton, a member of the Hodder Headline Group. All rights reserved. 'NIV' is a registered trademark of International Bible Society. UK trademark number 1448790.

First published 2001

British Library Cataloguing in Publication Data
A catalogue record for this book is available from the British Library.

ISBN 0-85111-545-4

Set in Adobe Garamond 11/13pt
Typeset in Great Britain
Printed in Great Britain by Creative Print and Design (Wales), Ebbw Vale

Inter-Varsity Press is the publishing division of the Universities and Colleges Christian Fellowship (formerly the Inter-Varsity Fellowship), a student movement linking Christian Unions in universities and colleges throughout Great Britain, and a member movement of the International Fellowship of Evangelical Students. For more information about local and national activities write to UCCF, 38 De Montfort Street, Leicester LE1 7GP, email@uccf.org.uk, or visit the UCCF website at www.uccf.org.uk.

'To the blind, all things are sudden'

William James

To the memory
of my good friend
Peter Livesey
and to
Sally, Davy and Josie

Contents

Foreword 9

Preface 11

Introduction 13

Chapter One
Making culture visible
21

Chapter Two
Our shrinking world
35

Chapter Three
Truth on trial
51

Chapter Four
Living with ourselves
69

Chapter Five
Living in relationship
85

Chapter Six
Living in a political community
104

Chapter Seven
The impact of technological change
133

Chapter Eight
The Spirit working in us
154

Postscript 179

Notes 184

FOREWORD

I walked into a house once where eighty-two people had been dragged from beneath the dining-room floor. They were murdered more than a month before, victims of a wicked religious cult. The house was perched charmingly at the top of a lush, green hill above the village of Rugazi in Uganda. Yet we felt we could almost touch the evil: it was a living presence that rode in on the breeze. Chiefly I remember the sickly stench of death. The producer and cameraman did the same as me: pressed handkerchiefs to our faces to avoid vomiting. Prisoners from the local jail had been forced to work, without shoes or gloves, unbelievably, to lift the bodies out.

So where did this tragedy come from? What gave birth to it? The leaders of the Movement for the Restoration of the Ten Commandments had promised their disciples a gilt-edged stake in the kingdom of God, enjoining them to live in the presence of the future – I'm sure that was the phrase they used – by signing over all possessions and denying the here and now. When the new millennium broke without the promised end of the world, some followers asked for their property back.

Panicking, the leaders killed and killed and killed. Disciples were quietly brought to the house for prayer in groups of three, then drugged and strangled. Then their bodies were dropped through a hole below the carpet. In the end more than a thousand Ugandans died, many locked inside a burning church. So much for living in the future. They weren't even allowed the present.

The four leaders had used the most powerful formula imaginable to reel in their victims – pretending to offer an uncompromised spirituality that speaks in the present tense. At any given moment, vast numbers of people are searching for exactly that. The cult exploited the confusion and the need.

No wonder religion gets a hammering from all and sundry. It's not easy to find a place for it in the twenty-first century; hard to justify even booking cupboard space when a self-styled Ten Commandments Movement turns gospel into slaughter. Why bother with religion when it can be melted down so easily for poison – and above all, how does a faith born 2,000 years ago stack up in a world where, as Roy points out, the newest waitress in one Soho restaurant is a three feet high stainless steel cube on rubber wheels?

Reading Roy McCloughry's book I found myself recalling the scene at the top of the hill. We need clear-sighted guidance like this to help us make sense of the future, and to help us see through the false promises self-appointed prophets.

Roy has written a timely and important account of Christianity in the world of text messaging and DVD, asking what the Bible can possibly say about life, the universe, and everything twenty-first century. 'The world in which we live is becoming increasingly enamoured of its own power,' he writes. The impact of technology on what we believe, the role of government, the dramatic redrawing of the political map – all are in the frame in Roy's analysis. The Ugandan cult offered a horrible lesson about the extent of the disarray that modern life has visited upon traditional faith; the world doesn't need another Movement for the Restoration of the Ten Commandments. But it can use a book like this.

Jeremy Vine

PREFACE

This book originated from the London Lectures in Contemporary Christianity delivered in 1996. I was honoured to be asked to give them under the title 'The spirit of the age: Christianity and the future of our culture', having attended the very first London Lectures as a student. I am grateful to the patrons of the London Lectures for their generosity in making the lectures possible at all. I am also grateful to the Bible Society for their willingness to finance the research that went into the compilation of the lectures.

A small group of friends met with me at the University of Nottingham over the year before the lectures to discuss some of the issues with which I was grappling. I would like to thank Prof. Roger Murphy, Dr Elizabeth Murphy, Rev. Georgina Morley, Rev. Roly Riems, Dr Martin Offord, Ms Ruth Layzell, Dr Christine Hall, Mr Peter McGavin and Helen McCloughry for their time as well as their patience with me. I would also like to thank those who chaired the lectures in London: Rev. Graham Cray, Rev. Dr Derek Tidball, Rev. Dr Martin Robinson and Mrs Elaine Storkey. Many people made constructive comments about the lectures at the time, and I received a number of invitations to repeat them in one form or another in the years following. They were replicated in Nottingham, and also formed the basis of the inaugural Birmingham Lecture in Contemporary Christianity. The Keswick Convention then asked me to deliver the inaugural Keswick Lectures on the State of the Nation and the State of the Church, and I was delighted to accept.

An invitation from my friend Lars Johansson to return to teach at Orebrö Seminary in Sweden gave me an opportunity to develop the lectures further. Finally, two visits to the Ukraine lecturing for the CCX (the Ukrainian member movement of the International Fellowship of Evangelical Students), and at the Centre for Leadership Development in Kiev enabled me to teach in a cultural context very different from the one I was describing. The chapter on technology would not have been added were it not for an invitation from Dr Derek Tidball, Principal of London Bible College, to deliver a paper at a conference on technology and theology held there in 1999, as well as an invitation from Nigel Williams, Director of Childnet International, to give a paper on internet ethics to its staff and trustees. Much of the book is underpinned by my experience of conducting over thirty interviews with cultural and political leaders for *Third Way* magazine, and I am grateful to Huw Spanner, its publisher, for his faith in my skills as an interviewer. Over this period I have been offered generous hospitality by people who have always been willing to debate and discuss, sometimes well into the night.

I am grateful also to Mark Greene, Director of the London Institute for Contemporary Christianity, for an invitation to give seven lectures on globalization during autumn 2000. They took place despite train disruptions and floods. Those lectures led to the insertion of chapter 2, which I hope will be helpful in putting the rest of the book into a wider context.

Dr Esther Eliot was the researcher on this project, and her acute theological mind was indispensable. Sarah Holt, Dr Kaja Ziesler, Emma Torrance and Charlotte Meldrum gave me invaluable assistance at the Kingdom Trust. The Trustees, Peter Ellis, Martyn Eden, Wendy Sayers, Alistair Turner, Richard Farrell and Steve Silvester, were supportive throughout the project. Many thanks to them. As ever, I would like to thank Helen, my wife, as well as Joanna, Lizzie and Lauren for their love and support throughout this whole project. Without them it would never have seen the light of day.

Roy McCloughry

Introduction

Living in the presence of the future

What kind of future do we want? Perhaps we don't want to know. We would rather be ignorant of the future. Let it take care of itself. Live for today. Or perhaps we are anxious. We live our lives expecting the worst, and in our anxiety we can see it coming nearer. Financial ruin, ill-health and ecological disaster are all possibilities which seem so likely to happen that they can rob us of our peace of mind.

The way we face the future influences the way we live today, and the way we live today influences our future. Are we optimists or pessimists about the future? Do we think we can control it in any way, or not? Perhaps, as for Eeyore, a character in the children's stories about Winnie-the-Pooh, all is gloom. Nothing will convince him that the future will be any different. Alternatively, millions of people in Britain do the National Lottery every week, believing that this time next week they might be millionaires, despite the fact that, statistically, they are more likely to be killed crossing the road to buy their ticket than to win the jackpot. For them the future is a land of opportunity. But whether the future is a foreign country or a familiar friend, we all have to come to terms with it in some way.

We live in a world of such rapid change that the idea that things will be different in the future is one of our culture's most basic assumptions. Of course, some things will never change. But what are they? A few years ago I might have written, 'For instance, what it means to be human will not change.' But now we are facing such a revolution in the areas of biotechnology and genetics that we are not so sure. Rapid change is both a blessing and a curse on our lives. Constantly adjusting to the presence of the future is stressful. Even as we weave miracles out of scarce resources we find ourselves living with less certainty and having to face up to the unintended consequences of our own actions. How different from the medieval world, where the lives of ordinary people did not change much, and where tradition was the conduit of both wisdom and foolishness from one generation to another! Now we are more interested in information than in wisdom, and assume that the knowledge of our parents' generation is irrelevant to our own experience. After all, we live in a world that is changing so fast that as soon as we get our new computer home and take it out of its box, it is out of date.

So how do we picture the future? Sociologist Graham May outlines four possible metaphors.[1] Perhaps we think of the future as a rollercoaster. The track twists round, and we can see only a little of it at a time. We cannot do anything about it, as we are strapped in. Or perhaps the future is a mighty river, sweeping us before it. It can be changed only by massive events such as natural disasters or by concerted human effort. We can ride it like whitewater rafters, with greater or lesser success, but our efforts to change it have no more effect than throwing pebbles into it. Maybe we think of the future as a huge ocean, with many possible destinations and routes to get to them. If we navigate well and avoid disasters, we shall reach our chosen destination, or we may change tack to go to a different one. Lastly, perhaps the future is a game of dice. Every second, millions of things happen; if they had not happened, the future would have been different. Everything is chance. All we can do is play the game and hope to be lucky.

Is the future more like a rollercoaster, a river, an ocean or a game? Each of them has different elements of life built into it. Where we have control, our expectations and our willingness to take risks are important. Where we have no control, we have to come to terms with being passive. Where we are myopic, we find it difficult to plan. Where everything is determined for us, we find our dignity compromised and feel like part of a cosmic machine. If the future is about chance, what responsibilities do we have? Why bother to invest in our future if everything is a game? So our view of the future as about risk, determinism, passivity, expectation or chance is important. It may be, of course, that each picture contains an element of truth or is more appropriate in some contexts than in others.

Of course, some people do not think they have a future. They have given up looking to it, planning for it or investing in it. Young people who face unemployment, those who are contemplating suicide or are mentally ill, or those with a terminal illness, may be among those who see themselves as facing a life without a future. Such an assumption, in whatever form it comes, has a marked impact on how they live now. Sometimes those living with HIV infection find it difficult when, having lived in the light of their imminent death, they are told they are now likely to live for some time as a result of successful drug therapy. They have made adjustments to their lives in the light of their death, and now become restless and confused about what to do with the new lease of life they have been given.

Although we all have personal ways of facing the future, we are increasingly aware of our need to face up to global futures as a human species. Adjustments to the present in the light of the future have been called for with respect to global projections. In recent years we have become accustomed to discussions of environmental, demographic, political and economic changes on a global scale. Global optimism or pessimism about the future of the planet has become a major industry, and it has had a huge impact on our collective imagination about our global future. One of the major issues in this context is whether we can do anything about the problems we face that will have an influence on what we perceive to be our future. In recent decades there have been a steadily increasing number of scientific conclusions that we have harmed the planet's ecosystems through the way we have lived over the last 200 years. The depletion of the ozone layer, the destruction of rain forests and of flora and fauna, pollution and soil erosion are laid out for us as reasons for the difficult future we are facing.

Is the river metaphor applicable here? We created the catastrophe, but do we now have the power to repair the damage? The governments of the world have signed treaties committing themselves to concerted action, but many countries have not followed through on their promises. Perhaps the future *is* already determined by past actions, and we have to reap the whirlwind.

Some reject this pessimistic scenario, citing different data, questioning the interpretations of others, and illustrating as they do so the way constant debate reflects our uncertainty about the future, even in a highly scientific age. Meanwhile, we continue to recycle our soft-drink cans, even though we damage the planet more by driving to the recycling point.

In business and planning it is predictions that are being paid for. Yet the track record of those who attempt to predict the future is not good. Economist Frank Paish once characterized economic forecasting as being like driving a car, in which policy-makers drive by looking in the rear mirror through the back window (relying on past data), with the windscreen blacked out (data about the present will not arrive for some months), and with the brake and accelerator pedals operating only with a lag of some months (policy takes time to have an effect). The trick is to accelerate when the economy is going downhill and brake when it is going uphill, so that the policy is timed to coincide with the right part of the business cycle (assuming we understand its behaviour correctly). Of course, recent history is littered with policy mistakes which caused the economy to overheat or to go into recession. Policy was timed wrongly, data were interpreted incorrectly or action was taken which was either too strong or too weak in its impact.

So much for personal and global futures. A Christian approach to the future seems to be completely different from these. In many ways it is, in that it is religious, rather than psychological or scientific. But these other approaches feed into a cultural worldview with which we have an interactive relationship. Even those people who are not religious may be surprised by the extent to which their view of the world has been affected by Christian perspectives.

Within a Christian worldview there seems to be scope for both optimism and pessimism. On the one hand, there is literature within the Bible which is apocalyptic in its focus. The world is going to end, and its end will be a disaster. It will disappear because it has been fatally compromised, not only morally, but because it does not reflect God's intentions for creation. A new world will be created, in which God's purposes will be reflected not only morally but environmentally as well. On the other hand, a strong theme of hope runs through the Bible. In the resurrection God has said 'yes' to creation. It is world-affirming rather than world-denying. In this world we are called to work, reflecting God the worker, and to manage the world on God's behalf.

Yet these two themes are not jumping-off points for optimism or pessimism. It is all too easy to use the Bible to confirm our own predilections or personality traits. A Christian view of the future arises out of Christian history; the way in which the coming of Christ has changed the world. He came to inaugurate the kingdom of God, that new world which is now invisible and lived in by faith, but which will one day be the visible presence or reign of God. To live as a Christian is to live within the kingdom of God and to have a primary allegiance to Christ as the ruler of heaven and earth. The presence of the kingdom of God brings with it both hope for the world and judgment upon the world. Both stem from the same event, the resurrection of Jesus from the dead. That event brought about both hope, because Christ defeated death, and judgment on all that is dead or speaks of death, because a new life has begun in which death and decay have no part.

If our view of the future is to be essentially Christian, it must be rooted in the resurrection and in a belief that the future is in God's hands. God is not surprised by the future, as we are. If we ignore this fact, we may feel at liberty to replace the Christian hope by optimism, fuelled perhaps by a misplaced faith in progress, and to jettison a Christian view of judgment in favour of a pessimism that emphasizes our powerlessness to change the future. Neither could be further from the truth. The future of the world is determined by an event that has already happened, the resurrection of Jesus Christ. At the moment, we, the church, are waiting for the full implications of that event to become visible in the life of the world. Whatever happens to the world, we always live with that knowledge.

At any point in time, hope and judgment are intertwined in a way that cannot be separated until the kingdom becomes visible. All points in history have both elements present within them. Whatever the context, personal, social, political or environmental, both are always present. This liberates us to look at the world with wisdom rather than with bias. It will always be the case that disasters occur, economies decline or diseases threaten life. But it is also the case that healthy communities are reborn, economies emerge from decline, and ways of conquering disease are found.

A Christian response to the world has four voices.[2] Firstly, we are the voice of *responsibility* for the world. We are to work as trustees of God's world to ensure that it remains fruitful and sustainable. This mandate not only is environmental but also entails maintaining all that God has provided to enable us to live healthy lives, such as the family and the community. As citizens, we are also to fulfil our obligations to ensure that people's rights are respected and that we live out our responsibilities to one another. Maintaining justice is an important part of our trusteeship.

Secondly, we are the voice of *celebration* in the world. We express blessing and praise, calling the world's attention to the good, the peaceable and the beautiful. We are those who delight in the world, its arts, music, and indeed all that is good. We try to refocus weary eyes on the clear and simple things of life, and lift up the heads of those who are so bowed down that they have forgotten about worship.

Thirdly, we are the voice of *prophecy* to the world. We are to be uncompromising about all that is contrary to God's purposes, whether poverty, debt slavery, moral evil or social decadence. Christians are therefore called to be the voice of prophecy, of resistance in an unjust society, and this may sometimes mean declaring that God is judge of the world. The church is not exempt from the impact of such declarations on its own life.

Fourthly, we are the voice of *suffering* to the world. We identify with those who suffer, realizing that we ourselves are not exempt from suffering in a world that has rejected Christ. We care not only for Christians, but for all who suffer, whatever their culture or religion.

So the church's four voices are responsibility for the world, celebration of the world, prophecy to the world and suffering with the world. In facing the future, Christians are called to make these things visible where they are invisible. This does not mean that we have any greater insight than others into the details of what will happen in the future; we are all subject to the ever-accelerating pace of change in our society and are trying to cope with its impact on our lives. But it does mean that we can learn from patterns of past biblical events, even if we cannot replicate them. Much can be learned from the history of Judeo-Christianity that will help us in our responsibilities in the future. We can see how God has dealt with situations in the past, and, if we are wise about the way we are living now, we may be able to offer something to our communities about the consequences for the future. As we shall see in the final chapter, the church is called to live this out in different cultural settings. This book attempts to look at how we might live in our own cultural context.

It all comes down to what kind of future we are talking about. If we mean predicting the future with certainty, our experience of the past tells us that we are unlikely to be able to do that. But if we mean understanding our future, the Christian narrative has much insight to offer us – so much so that to the extent that we abandon that narrative, we not only lose our understanding of our present condition, we also face an incomprehensible future.

Such a view leads us to the stances taken throughout this book. They are summed up in the three words *recognition*, *reflection* and *action*. First, most of us look at the future not objectively, but subjectively. We are not called to predict trends or to ask what scientific research will make possible in the next decade. But we do have a subjective view of the future based on our experience, our education and our own reading of the world. The problem is that our information comes from the past. But from time to time we receive new information about what is going on in the world, and we have an experience of recognition. For us, this information about our contemporary condition is news from the future. Within this book I hope that some people will find a point of recognition, opening up new possibilities for them. For most of us, recognition is far more important than prediction, as it is part of understanding the world, and that in turn is related to wisdom which, as we shall see, is at a premium in our society. Others, of course, will read this book and find nothing new. They are already aware of everything in its pages and have incorporated it into their worldview. They are looking in a different direction for information that will enable them to understand that combination of the present and the future that recognition brings.

Secondly, recognition brings both the possibility of reflection and the responsibility to reflect. We may not be able to predict the future, but we can reflect upon it. To avoid doing so displays a lack of concern about the consequences of our actions, either personal or social. Without reflection, we are condemned to repeating our mistakes over and over again. Reflection on the unintentional consequences of our actions is particularly important.

Thirdly, we are called to action. By 'action' I do not mean 'activism'. For instance, reflecting upon the nature of our relationships may mean that we decide to become *less* busy in order to give more time to others. Prayer also is action, as is hospitality, and both require us to create space for others and to lay down other responsibilities. Yet those with responsibilities in churches are all too aware that a few people are doing the job of the many, and that those who do nothing need to face up to their responsibility to become more active in the church or in the community. Christian action is always most effective when it is founded on Christ's calling to be faithful to his commands. There is a great gulf between being effective in our witness and capitulating to the current obsession with efficiency, which constantly urges us to do more with the resources at our disposal, and which can quickly take over our lives rather than enabling us to serve others.

1
Making culture visible

The term 'culture' does not necessarily refer to the world of fine art and 'high-brow' literature, although they are expressions of it. Soap opera is as much a part of our culture as Covent Garden opera. 'Culture' describes the world we have built out of our assumptions, beliefs and actions, and which finds its concrete form in the institutions, events, attitudes and trends with which we live. These, in turn, point to the meanings and purposes of our lives. We create culture together, but in turn it shapes us. It expresses the worldviews we hold and is the lens through which the world comes into focus. When we compare cultures, we see how their institutions, patterns of social behaviour, relationships and religious beliefs express their different perceptions of the world.

Many elements of our own culture are invisible to us. The old adage 'a fish discovers water last' indicates that it is difficult to 'see' our own culture objectively. It is often when we meet people from other cultures, or travel abroad ourselves, that we become aware that our own worldview is not as normal, neutral or natural as we may have supposed. For example, many of us become conscious of our accent only when we move away from our locality to study or work, and find ourselves talking differently from those around us. Culture is 'the way we do things around here'.

If we are uncritical of our own worldview, it can become a hidden standard of measurement by which we judge the views and behaviour of others. People are found wanting, not because of any inherent weaknesses in their beliefs or their institutions, but simply because they are different from us. We may then excuse behaviour in ourselves that we condemn in others. The last century saw terrible oppression which arose from the belief that one culture had the right to impose itself on others by the use of military force because it was superior.

It is easy to make assumptions about those who are different from us, thereby reinforcing false stereotypes and perpetuating a climate of blame. People become socially excluded when their voice is not heard and they are prevented from entering into the dialogue that lies at the heart of any free society. It is all too easy to assume that they are the ones with the problem and therefore they are the ones who must change. But if we are to be a truly open society, we must listen most carefully to the criticisms of those who are dissatisfied and disenfranchized.

Many of the aspects of our culture that are most powerful in our lives are invisible to us. We see through them like a window; we do not notice them or their power. Consequently, we are unable to evaluate them. We can neither celebrate them nor repent of them. While this situation remains, any statement we might make about being committed to 'truth' or 'justice' must ring hollow. We must be prepared to make the invisibility of our own culture visible and to deal with what we find.

Consider the change in attitude that has occurred in Britain through the Stephen Lawrence affair. A young black man was brutally murdered on the street. It was only after years of lobbying by his family, and following a police investigation characterized by incompetence and prejudice, that a report found that there was institutional racism in some parts of the police force. It is so easy to ignore the very messages we need to hear the most. We can learn only when we listen, and we will listen only when we become aware that a healthy community life depends on openness to the views of others, however painful it may be to hear them. Willingness to change ourselves is a far more robust indicator of a healthy society than a desire to change others.

In the latter half of the twentieth century the relationship between Christianity and culture brought to a head changes that have been taking place over hundreds of years. Whatever the private beliefs of the population, Christianity is no longer seen as an expression of public culture. One view, frequently represented in the media, holds that believing in one true God makes Christianity a threat to pluralism. From this perspective it is a short distance to labelling Christianity as a source of intolerance or even of arrogance. At the same time there is an extraordinary amount of ignorance about Christianity. It sometimes appears that Christianity is in the line of fire in a way other religions are not.

Ironically, the very same media often debate the loss of moral leadership in our society and frequently criticize church leaders for not giving a lead. When leaders become fearful of raising their heads above the parapet in case they are labelled intolerant, they, and the churches they lead, are quickly labelled inconsequential and therefore irrelevant to the struggles of contemporary culture. What has happened is that the church is now heard on the world's terms. When it speaks of God's love for all, it can be heard, because it seems to pose no threat to anybody. Love is interpreted as unconditional acceptance and blanket tolerance. But when the church speaks of God's holy character and his moral demands, this is regarded as unacceptable intolerance. This tension between unconditional tolerance and unacceptable intolerance runs through our culture like lettering through a stick of rock. The attempt to divide love from holiness would be immediately recognized by Amos or Isaiah. It is a strategy adopted over millennia to smother the prophetic voice.

Yet this change has led the church to re-examine the extent to which its views are distinctive from those outside the church. If its views are synonymous with those of the culture, it cannot be a missionary church, as it has no message to convey. Under such scrutiny, liberal theology has withered because its Christianized humanism has had little to offer. Evangelical churches have prospered, not only because of their representation of the Christian tradition and their enthusiasm for mission, but also, most recently, because of their willingness to engage with contemporary culture. Of course, Christians hold theological doctrines about salvation, the incarnation and the character of God. But Christianity also has distinctive contributions to make to debates about politics, economics, gender and technology. Our society often forgets the extent to which it owes its heritage to its Christian past. So much that is good in our culture is rooted in our Christian past or in its current influence. It is all too easy to focus on the horrors of bloody religious wars and the catalogue of violence which has resulted from the abuse of religious power. It is also easy to ignore that in the twentieth century, the most secular of all centuries, more people were killed violently than in the rest of human history.

This book's attempt to show that Christian thinking is distinctive is an attempt to make something visible again that has become invisible. It is the hope of Christians that the recovery of a Christian worldview, which is an integrated part of life rather than something contained in a separate religious compartment, will bring about the transformation of our society. Yet this is only worth attempting if Christianity is in fact a guarantor of a free and open society rather than a threat to it. Christian truth should be the basis of freedom, not of authoritarianism. If Christianity is true, we have nothing to fear from open debate or from scrutiny of our positions. True tolerance, which is so essential to any free society, depends on genuine engagement.

But are those of us who are Christians willing to face up to our own failures? If we are not, our claim to regard truth as important will be laughed out of court. There are cultures where Christianity is growing rapidly and affecting the public life of nations. So what has happened in the West? Why, despite the fact that the majority of people in the United States call themselves Christians, is that country such a source of violence, materialism and sexual licence? These are sombre questions for the church. How can a church that is losing thousands of people out of its back door every week claim to have the answer to life's deepest questions? Those people obviously didn't think so. Even as we attempt to create a distinctive Christian worldview which is relevant to the twenty-first century, we have to be honest about the struggles we are having within the church. Honesty, integrity and transparency are a vital but sometimes painful part of Christian witness. We cannot assume that those in the church have a worldview entirely separate from those outside it. We are all affected by way we live in our society. That is why it is so important to make the society's thinking visible and to contrast it with Christian teaching. Otherwise Christian discipleship will be reduced to church attendance, with no transformation of our lives.

Culture and creation

Is there any distinctive way in which Christianity has viewed the process of interaction with the surrounding culture? Not surprisingly, we find ourselves starting with Judeo-Christian ideas of the creation of the world. These try to come to terms with the relationship between God, humanity and the world, and therefore have to wrestle with the relationship between Christianity and culture.

When Christians ask questions about culture, they base them on an understanding of creation. However those questions are answered (and there is no one way of answering them), there is no escaping the centrality of God as creator in a Christian approach to culture. It is simply not possible to plunge into a discussion about culture based on 'rights' or 'aesthetics' without first making that clear. Yet any discussion in which that is done will quickly establish the distinctiveness of any Christian position and the fact that current debates about culture have abandoned a Christian worldview.

One of the weaknesses of our view of creation is that all too often we see it only as a story about beginnings. It is as if we see the creation story as a launchpad from which the story of human history takes off. Once the rocket is launched, the launchpad is no longer needed. God made the world, and since then, although he is always present with us, he no longer seems present with us as creator. Yet creation is a continuous process. God is always creator, and that process continues throughout human history. God is committed to creation and is constantly interacting with it.

God is also committed to culture. There are two reasons for this. First, we are *embodied*. When God breathed into the person of dust, that person became a living being. This being was not divisible into body and spirit. In creating the human body, God gave it sacred significance. When Jesus was born in bodily form he said 'yes' to the body. In his resurrection he did not reject the body. It was transformed, but it was also a body that could still be touched or that could eat fish on a beach. When he was on earth he was limited, as we are, by experiencing life through the body. This shared experience is something to be celebrated. It gives us an assurance that our own acts of creation have significance, and that God is thus committed to culture.

God is constantly relating to us as creator in that bodily relationship. It follows that what we do with our bodies, the way we live with one another and the impact of our decisions on our communities are of acute concern to the creator, who relates to us, not once at the outset of time, but continuously throughout it. Our identity is not formed by our relationship with God in a static, once-for-all way. Our ongoing relationship with God as creator is a constant reminder that we are here not by chance but by a deliberate divine choice.

God relates to the world not only by creating it and being committed to it, but by continuing to renew and sustain it. As Jesus says, the Father is 'working still'. God affirmed creation by becoming incarnate in Jesus, who, in human form, embodies human action in himself. In Christ, God declares that we do not need to set aside the body in order to understand his purposes. Indeed, denying the body and our life together in favour of understanding religion as some disembodied calling causes a fundamental distortion in God's relationship with us. God's committed relationship to creation, through making it, sustaining it and becoming a part of it, demonstrates an intense absorption with human history in all its aspects.

The second reason God is committed to culture is that we are *embedded* in it. In other words, Christians cannot escape from culture. Whatever stance we take, we are deeply involved in the culture in which we live. But just as we try to escape from being embodied by attempting to divide body from spirit, so we also try to escape from being embedded in our culture by separating the church from the world. But this we cannot do. We are not to be of the world, but this is not the same as behaving as if the church could somehow live in isolation from culture, as if it were a desert island surrounded by water. We are called to influence our culture for Christ. Conversely, it is also necessary to allow the gospel to make visible the way in which culture is having an impact on us as Christians. Whether it is the impact of advertising, reactions to the social and political issues of the day or attitudes to our education and upbringing, we deal with these things as people embedded in culture.

Any tendency to spiritualize our Christian faith falsely will therefore mean that we tend to talk conceptually about life rather than taking into account the way in which people actually experience life through the body. Any tendency to separatism will deny us, as a church, the possibility of being an effective witness within our culture. One of the reasons this book grapples with issues such as gender and technology is that these have real significance for us as a culture, and we cannot escape their implications in our daily lives.

Creation and nature

God is also committed to the natural world. Ecological crises are of concern to a God who, in Christ, 'holds all things together'. Such problems remind us that we are stewards of the world and that ecological responsibility cannot be divorced from Christian responsibility. We cannot view the effects of technology as neutral, but are called to evaluate them in the light of all we know about God's purposes for the world. If we let God's commitment to creation float free from the difficult issues we are facing at the beginning of the twenty-first century, we abdicate our Christian responsibility to get involved in the struggle to preserve our environment. We have to see creation as nature.

But the opposite is also true. If, as a culture, we fail to see nature as creation, we lose sight of its value. This is what has happened in the modern world, which has lost the ability, or the desire, to look at nature and, by faith, see it as creation. If nature is creation, it is a thing of value, a call to worship its creator. If it is not, both it and we are diminished. A society that does not see nature as creation ends up by putting nature to death along with God. The Bible's picture of humanity's dominion over the earth was that of the shepherd king, the benevolent ruler who had the best interests of the world at heart. The replacement of this image by the idea of ownership, and the consequent weakening of our sense of accountability for our actions, moved us from dominion to domination. Our abuse of power, particularly in the pursuit of consumption, has affected every area of our environmental life.

In his Reith Lectures for 1999, sociologist Anthony Giddens talked of the way in which we now view nature and of the way this has affected our entire worldview. How, he asked, has taking control over nature affected us? Could it be that our attempt to control our own destiny has backfired on us? Whatever we have done, we have to face up to the unintended consequences of our actions. We are all aware that we are living with a world whose future seems less certain and whose behaviour seems riskier than it has ever done.

For Giddens, the idea of risk is a key to understanding the way we think about culture and nature in the modern world. Risk is a modern concept. Of course, life has always been subject to the hazards and uncertainties of natural disasters, illness or unemployment. The Middle Ages, according to Thomas Hobbes, were 'nasty, brutish, and short'. But Giddens says that there was no concept of risk, either in the Middle Ages or in other traditional cultures such as in Japan or China. Hazards were dealt with by reference to the will of God or to fate.

> Traditional cultures didn't have a concept of risk because they didn't need one. Risk isn't the same as hazard or danger. Risk refers to hazards that are actively assessed in relation to future possibilities. It comes into wide usage only in a society that is future oriented – which sees the future precisely as a territory to be conquered or colonised. Risk presumes a society that actively tries to break away from its past, the prime characteristic, indeed, of modern civilisation.[1]

Certainly the worldview of the Middle Ages saw the world as created by God, but it had welded that belief to the establishment of a religious hierarchy characterized by certainty and power. It was the job of the church to police a system whose rigidity meant that the ordinary person had little freedom to disagree with the accepted dogma of the day. The individual had little or no control in a society in which an élite held power. The collapse of that worldview meant the passing of a way of life in which meaning, certainty and power were combined. The Age of Reason placed power in the hands of individuals, who could exercise choice through the application of their own reason rather than being dominated by the will of others. Formerly, power was wielded by the few over the many, and the passing of the old system made the beginnings of a new way of life possible. But with the new freedom came new risks. Theologian Walter Brueggemann says of this:

> By 'meaning' I refer to a trusted set of symbols that in that period was constituted by Christian theology. By 'power' I mean the capacity to exercise economic and political control in legitimated ways. By linking the two, I refer to ... the neat fit of certitude and domination. As the certitude given by the Church synthesis began to weaken ... so the capacity to control also began to weaken. With the loss of certitude and the loss of domination, life was indeed at risk.[2]

These were traditional societies in which life changed little from generation to generation. In such societies, where the future looks much like the past, the concept of risk is eliminated. But when people believe they can control and shape the future, risk becomes very important. Risk is, of course, both positive and negative. People accomplish great feats through facing up to risk. Adventurers and explorers discover continents and climb mountains. Capitalism has developed through the willingness of investors to back new products and to trust those who trade with them. Indeed, as Giddens points out, western capitalism depends on estimating future profit and loss, which involves an assessment of risk. This is a world in which the risk assessment of nature has replaced the idea of a world created and sustained by God. Instead, the insurance industry finds its *raison d'être* in the balance between the risks of the future and the need for security in the future.

This is indeed a world where certainty and domination have passed away. We have moved from a world whose certainties indicated the powerlessness of the individual to a world whose uncertainties point to the use and abuse of power. Whereas we are familiar with what Giddens calls 'external risk' from earthquakes, floods or failed harvests, which was often thought of in religious terms, we are now concerned about 'manufactured risk'. What we have done to nature becomes more important than what nature can do to us.[3]

The rise of science as 'certain' knowledge and the weakening of religion's claims on certainty have had a marked impact on western culture. But science's former claim to objective knowledge is now seen as suspect. One of the hallmarks of our culture at the outset of the new millennium is an awareness of the fragility of scientific knowledge and a suspicion of its analysis. For example, there is confusion over whether genetically modified foods are a good thing. Meanwhile, GM crops continue to be grown in bulk in North America. Perhaps we have intervened in nature to such an extent that we have arrived at what Anthony Giddens calls 'the end of nature':

> Our society lives after the end of nature. The end of nature doesn't mean, obviously, that the physical world or physical processes cease to exist. It refers to the fact that there are few aspects of our surrounding material environment that haven't been affected in some way by human intervention. Much of what used to be natural isn't completely natural any more, although we can't always be sure where the one stops and the other begins.[4]

These issues are not just related to discussion of the physical world. We are caught up in a maelstrom of changing cultural opinions, the marginalizing of traditions which once guided us, and media portrayal of an infinite number of consumer choices. In all this, we are faced with daily choices which mean that we are all living with risk and uncertainty in every area of our lives. This is one explanation why, even though western Christians are necessarily caught up in this by virtue of being members of their culture, the knowledge that God is a God of love is essential to our security. It enables us to have a view of the future which is based, not on risk assessment, but on the resurrection, which is God's affirmation of creation.

With hindsight it is easy to criticize the ideas at the heart of the Age of Reason, and Christians have done so frequently with good cause. As Lesslie Newbigin has said, however, 'the light of the Enlightenment was real light'.[5] Few people would want to go back to pre-modern times or look on them nostalgically. We do not want to deny the value of the many advances that have come about through the application of human reason to the problems that face the world.

Yet the Enlightenment gave rise to new problems by divorcing reason from the existence of God, since it is through our awareness of being created beings that we are able to live within the limits God has set for us. The denial of those limits means that it is no longer possible to give account to God for our stewardship of creation, since we are living in a world that is increasingly out of control. Like parents who have abused their children, and are apprehensive lest they turn on them and harm them, we fear the effects of our own abuse of nature.

Perhaps it is western culture that should bear most responsibility for the creation of a world at risk. Those who are powerful must bear responsibility for the abuse of power. As globalization, driven by western markets, creates new opportunities across the world, it exports new risks. Yet many still believe that, despite this, western culture should become universal, since liberal democracy, an export of the West, is the best system for organizing civil society. Others see this as arrogance. The fact that western products are consumed throughout the world, or that western films are watched around the world, does not mean that the cultures that consume them are becoming westernized. Some are hostile to the West. The fact that English has become a universal language does not prove that all cultures are merging into western culture. English is a way of communicating, rather than a source of identity. Perhaps this belief that modernization must mean westernization demonstrates that our own culture is invisible to us and highlights our ignorance of other cultures around the world. But they have strengths, from which we can learn. As many commentators have noted, what we regard as universal other cultures see as western, and many want nothing to do with it, preferring to seek some other way.

Certainly, exporting the weaknesses of the West will wreak havoc in other cultures. After all, where are we now? South African theologian David Bosch has said:

> The illusion that human hopes for freedom, justice and true progress can be realized by relying on reason or human resolve alone, or by the mechanics of economic, technological or political development, has finally exploded. Enlightenment reason, which had declared itself autonomous and had conferred legitimacy upon itself, is now being challenged to

defend its legitimacy. But this it cannot do, for a rational process left to itself resembles a self-propelling machine the functioning of which no longer stands under the control of a purpose.[6]

Journalist Clifford Longley once put it in this way:

Western civilisation suffers from a strong sense of moral and spiritual exhaustion. Having constructed a society of unprecedented sophistication, convenience and prosperity, nobody can remember what it was supposed to be for. Just enjoying it does not seem to enough. Indeed enjoyment as an end in itself quickly turns to ashes in the mouth. Not only is it boringly bland. It is even more boringly purposeless. There is more to human life than comfort, entertainment and the avoidance of suffering.[7]

A postmodern culture?

Just as the export of the scientific, political and economic wonders of the modern world was becoming possible, a new set of influences was emerging, which have become known as *postmodern*. The word 'postmodern' raises the question whether the modern world is passing away, or whether this is just another phase of the modern world. If 'modern' means 'just now', how can something be 'after just now'? What it describes has no identity of its own, for it is 'post'. It may be 'after' modernity, but it is still firmly attached to the modern world. Malcolm Bradbury argued that it would take the beginning of a new millennium to push it (whatever it is) into an identity of its own.[8]

The history of the world is a history of the birth and death of great cultures. Is ours dying? In decades to come, will we witness the death of the West and the dominance of Chinese or Islamic civilizations? We cannot be sure. What we do know is that our version of the modern world is no longer unique. It is difficult to talk about 'modernity' in the singular any more. Other nations and cultures have become industrialized and now form part of the global market, but from backgrounds very different from our own. Japan may be modern, but its culture is hardly rooted in Christianity.

The word 'postmodern' has been used in art and architecture for many years. But in recent years it has come into popular usage. Postmodernity is a criticism of the modern world, raising the kinds of objection we noted in the previous section. But it may also mark the birth of a new kind of society with worldviews different from those with which we are currently familiar. Behind the ideas of postmodernism we find thinkers such as Friedrich Nietzsche, who was severely critical of modern hopes and pronounced the death of God. If God is dead, what can we know with any certainty? Maybe there are multiple realities. Postmodernity questions how far science is based on observable facts. The local replaces universal concepts of knowledge. The culture of words, arguments and printed books becomes exchanged for the image and the screen. No objective meaning exists beyond language. Language floats free from the world; symbols begin to refer to each other rather than to anything rooted in objective reality. History is irrelevant; the future is unknown. We live in the eternal present. Life becomes a series of leisure opportunities based on consumption. Knowledge as we know it disappears. Trust goes. Anything goes.

Over the last few hundred years our changing culture has experimented with different approaches to meaning. There are three in particular, related to the pre-modern, modern and postmodern ages. The first approach was *dogmatism*, which, as we have seen, attempted to combine certainty with power. The second was *scepticism*, which made it possible to ask questions about the world without fear of adverse consequences should the answers, or the absence of answers, displease the religious or political authorities. The pursuit of scepticism as a method, however, meant that it was only a matter of time before it turned on itself. Scepticism may have given birth to the modern world, but it has also threatened its continued existence. It may have originally been used to release people from religious oppression, but now it is used to question the consequences of human liberation.

This sequence has brought us to the third attitude to meaning, which is *cynicism*. It can be transitional and particular, in that when something in which we invested our beliefs collapses we are left deflated and disillusioned, but still aware that this phase in our lives will pass. Or it can become a habit which is so ingrained in the cultural imagination that it appears to be entirely acceptable and, indeed, the very apotheosis of sophisticated analysis. Although many aspects of postmodernity should be welcomed and celebrated, there has been an increasing acceptance of cynicism over the last decade, particularly in the English media. Ironically, cynicism is not a sceptical attitude to meaning but a dogmatic subversion of meaning. By only attacking others, cynics hide from the goodness of the world. The Christian practice of faith, hope and love aims to heal that which is self-destructive in our culture. But this mission must be put in a cultural context. Without an understanding of that context, we shall be unable to recognize or reflect on the significance of faith, hope and love for the culture in which we live. It is also the case that, as we shall see, western Christianity may have become dependent on modernity. If this is so, then the advent of a postmodern world may prove to be necessary to the renewal of the Christian faith.

Postmodernity is not just about ideas, but about the processes through which the world is being transformed. Our culture is being changed not only from within, but by a vast array of interconnected global forces. It is to this process of globalization that we now turn.

2
Our shrinking world

The end of the twentieth century was heralded by the implosion of communism in 1989. Since then, new markets have been opening up all over the world. In fact, the world is becoming a series of vast, interconnected markets. At the same time the growth of the internet means that we are becoming increasingly aware that we are living in a shared space. We live with the consequences of the decision-making of those who live elsewhere in the world, with whom we have no relationship and over whom we have no authority. A new industry opens in Liverpool or closes in Glasgow because of decisions made in Hanover, Hong Kong or Bangkok rather than in the boardrooms of British companies.

Globalization: winners and losers

Globalization has been defined as 'the widening, deepening and speeding up of worldwide interconnectedness in all aspects of contemporary social life, from the cultural to the criminal, the financial to the spiritual'.[1] It describes the impact of the media, the growth of migration, the development of tourism and the challenges of environmental degradation. It also describes the process by which the relationship between nation-states, international agencies and multinational corporations is changing all the time. For some, this is a source of inspiration and optimism, since there is much in the world that can be changed for the better. Globalization will, according to them, produce high and converging incomes throughout the world. Poor nations will have greater access to markets and will be able to wean themselves off aid as they sell their products in global markets. Access to the internet will mean that everybody can find those markets easily and can also acquire education and knowledge in a way that has not been possible until now. This new economy will be stimulating and imaginative. Driven by competition, it will stimulate ideas. Of course, many of the old ways of working will disappear, but many of them, especially the unskilled manual jobs, were not worth preserving. Surely it is better to let technology take the strain, or even to transfer those jobs to the developing world, where they provide a welcome source of income and a stepping-stone to greater things? Optimists are most excited about the liberalization of trade, the benefits of information technology and the opportunities for wealth creation they offer.

They point out that the age during which we thought of 'the West and the rest' is over. What took countries like Britain a century to achieve has been compressed into three decades in many of the Asian countries. In 1962 South Korea had a gross domestic product per head similar to that of the Sudan. Today it is not far behind some of the nations of western Europe.[2] Martin Jacques comments:

> Asia is full of energy and hope: it is imbued with a culture of can-do, with an enormous appetite for change. Europe by way of contrast is dominated by a culture of can't-do, with every new challenge seen as a problem. Asia is like a lean and hungry adolescent, Europe quintessentially middle-aged.[3]

Whether this is a fair judgment or not, businesses in Europe are very aware of the competition they face from Asia. Workforces are becoming used to hearing that redundancy is due to the sourcing of goods from Asia because they are more competitive. But, for the optimists, although there will be winners and losers, the gains will outweigh the losses.

For others, the power of globalization brings with it a sense of fatalism, since it seems to challenge the power of national governments to control situations or to resist inappropriate change. It poses questions about the limits to politics as we currently know it. The pessimists see it as a process that increases the gap between the rich and the poor, and that delivers national interests into the hands of big business. It is certainly true that the gap between rich and poor is widening. The average income per head in Switzerland is now 400 times that in Mozambique. Protest against the international institutions at the heart of the world economy, such as the International Monetary Fund, the World Trade Organization and the World Bank, has led to violent demonstrations at their recent meetings in Seattle and Prague. Mention the word and feelings can run high. One of the groups that organized protest in Seattle stated that they had 'gathered together to express their opposition to the loss of democracy in the face of the overpowering onslaught of global corporate dominance'.[4] However, this is only one element in the matrix of change which is making the world a smaller place.

> Globalisation is not just about things such as the ratio of exports to gross domestic product. It has to do with the nonchalant way in which people under thirty make international telephone calls, the reaction of General Motors workers in Flint, Michigan, when Chrysler was bought by Daimler-Benz, the new cafés in Shanghai where you can get a decent cappuccino (and sometimes surf the Internet), the more or less instantaneous availability all over the world of Viagra and Harry Potter, the clothes people wear, or even the fact that in the Himalayan hamlet of Lukla people setting off for Mount Everest are given French toast and Swiss muesli for breakfast with soft toilet paper also on sale.[5]

In one sense globalization is nothing new. We know that worldwide Christian mission has itself been a major force in globalization as the gospel transformed cultures, forged links between nations and in many cases exported western culture as well. Economically, our world has been 'connected' for several hundred years. In the fourteenth century, German merchants traded iron and agricultural products across borders. Merchant adventurers based in the UK sold wool to the Low Countries, and by the end of the fourteenth century there were as many as 150 Italian banks operating internationally.[6] During the eighteenth and nineteenth centuries, great trading companies such as the Dutch and British East India Companies came into existence, and as the Industrial Revolution took hold many companies produced goods which were sold throughout the colonies. New techniques of production, management and distribution meant that companies became truly 'multinational' from around 1870 and by the First World War those trading patterns were firmly established. Through the twentieth century 'connexity' intensified. But the fact that globalization is not new has not stifled what has been called the 'gee whiz' response to the current situation, which sees the world as entering an entirely new phase of human development. For people with this view, we are facing changes which can only be compared to the onset of the Industrial Revolution.

In the twenty-first century, borders come down not so much because physical dividing-walls are dismantled but because there is no effective restriction on the free flow of information across borders. The information society has made it difficult for totalitarian regimes, such as Burma, to isolate their societies, since the internet can convey information around the world. So we face a situation in which the moral problems previously associated with the defence of the realm are now inextricably linked to those associated with the censorship of information.

Competition in our fast-changing world is technology-led. One of the possibly long-term problems we face is that of the relationship between technology and humanity, which is often confused and ambivalent. A technological society tends to represent human beings not as persons, but as resources. The dominant technological value, which is efficiency, is not suited to human beings, who are made for relationship. At our best, we are inefficient when compared to the capabilities of technology. Many people in the workforce today are working beyond their natural limits, and are experiencing stress because global technology's speed, capacity and omnipresence are too demanding. Our lives are being put under stress by an interconnected world that is at work twenty-four hours a day. Often it is the powerless who suffer most from this.

The financial markets

Markets convey globalization, and, like technology, have a marked impact on how we live. Globalization is primarily an economic phenomenon. It forces us to come to terms with the world after communism, in which capitalism has become more aggressive. The dominance of market-driven capitalism has meant a huge expansion of all kinds of markets throughout the world, with the number of stock markets in developing countries doubling in the 1990s. The volume of trading on the world's foreign-exchange markets has doubled since 1980. Yet there are fears that this rush of money throughout the world is making it a more fragile place. The stakes are high, but so are the risks of failure. The near collapse (albeit short-lived) of the Asian 'tiger' economies sent a warning to the financial markets that things could go wrong at a moment's notice. Speculative money enters the economies of developing countries in search of high returns, and when those returns begin to flag, money can swiftly exit in search of higher profit. The presence of corruption, ignored when profits are good, adds to the scramble to get out. An economy that is in the middle of a boom may then collapse. In a global economy, this can be a disaster not only for the country or region concerned, but also for those banks that lent the money in the first place. The massive capital flows moving across the world do not always follow the 'laws' of supply and demand learnt by economics students. Their direction owes as much to herd instinct as to rational assessment.

Many countries do not participate in the global economy. Some countries that have the infrastructure and goods to benefit, such as Mexico, Thailand, Brazil and Russia, can be so fragile that they go under in a major crisis. Yet many countries do not have access to global markets; they are not 'insiders'. Areas such as Sub-Saharan Africa miss out because of the absence of an educated labour force and efficient business systems, or the presence of corruption. Many African countries cannot attract investment because there is insufficient infrastructure to support the market. As global capitalism spreads wealth to some parts of the world, others grow poorer. Globalization intensifies those differences.

The relationship between free markets and social democracy is a disturbing one when viewed from a global perspective. For instance, countries that have a welfare state are competing with those that do not. The latter have much lower costs, and therefore can be attractive to investors because they can produce goods at a lower price. Can there be social justice when everything is traded on global markets? In this 'race to the bottom', markets demand goods made by those with the lowest wages, who have no trade-union representation, healthcare, pension opportunity or other benefits conferred by social democracy. The welfare state is, of course, a way of conferring economic benefits on people, but its roots are in a political commitment, an expression of the kind of society we want to live in. Globalization has a habit of depoliticizing issues, making them primarily economic. Are we happy with a society in which voters have less power than investors? We may now be a market economy, but do we want to become a market society?

The transformation of politics

Those who emphasize that we are in a completely new situation point out that in political terms we have moved from an international economy to a global one. The difference between these is that an international world conducts business between nations, but in a global world the nation-state has become one player among others, all of whom have power and influence.

Previously, the relationship between states followed the Westphalian model (derived from the Peace of Westphalia, 1648) in which Europe was divided into a number of sovereign states that recognized no superior authority. Each made its own laws and settled its own disputes. International law referred primarily to the rules necessary for their co-existence, and endorsed the right of each state to independent action. The growth of diplomacy forged links between states, but major differences between them were often settled by force.

Today, the situation has changed out of all recognition. We now live in a world in which the influence of states, multinationals and international non-governmental organizations (INGOs) all have an impact on global governance. Governments now voluntarily limit their sovereignty. Having signed human-rights charters, they cannot do what they like to their citizens any more. Since environmental problems cannot be contained within borders, nation-states have to co-operate to find solutions. International crime and information technology are powerful 'transboundary' forces that cannot be dealt with by any one state alone. These problems blur the distinction between the foreign and the domestic, internal political issues and external questions, the sovereign concerns of the nation-state and international considerations.

> States and governments face issues like AIDS, BSE (Bovine Spongiform Encephalopathy), the spread of malaria, the use of non-renewable resources, the management of nuclear waste, diaspora cultures and the proliferation of instruments of mass destruction which cannot easily be categorised in traditional political terms, that is domestic or international. Moreover, issues like the location and investment strategy of multinational corporations, the regulation of financial markets, the development of EMU [European Monetary Union] and the threat to the tax bases of individual countries which rise from the global division of labour and the absence of capital controls all pose questions about the continued effectiveness of some of the traditional instruments of economy policy.[7]

All of these are areas of transboundary concern in which governments are bound together in attempting what they cannot do on their own. Political communities now overlap and are no long independent from one another. This raises important issues for the existence of democracy. Later in the book we shall consider democracy further, but in the context of globalization particular questions arise. A wave of democratization has spread over the world since the collapse of communism. Since the Second World War, liberal democracy has increasingly become the dominant form of the state.

> In 1974 at least 68% of all countries could reasonably be called authoritarian; by the end of 1995, nearly 75% of all countries had established procedures for competitive elections and adopted some formal guarantees of political and civil rights.[8]

In a democracy, it is important that citizens are able, by means of the vote, to hold their political representatives to account. With that consent, politicians are then able to make laws to govern their constituents. The wave of democratisation has been one of the distinctives of globalization, but globalization also creates problems for democracy. How do we show our support for the government's stance on issues that lie outside the sole control of the nation-state? Governments govern by our consent, but are deeply involved in issues that are not easily defined. If many of the most important issues facing us have their source outside, or extend beyond, the traditional boundaries of the nation, we need to know how to vote in a way that enables us to be properly represented in those areas. It is not clear how this can be done. Many of these issues are resolved (if they can be resolved) by a process of bartering between many different kinds of agencies, including corporations, INGOs and IGOs (inter-governmental organizations). A government may have a policy but its influence on what happens may well be lost in that process.

One way in which EU citizens can express their wishes at a supranational level is by participating in elections to the European Parliament, where many of these issues are discussed. Yet low turnouts at European elections demonstrate the sense of alienation people have from that. Voters find it difficult to transfer to a regional body the loyalties they may feel towards their national politicians. This loyalty (itself fast diminishing, if the size of the poll is any indication) depends on a tradition that contributes a great deal to the nation's sense of identity. But the UK, in particular, struggles to identify with regional Europe.

At the very least, we have to admit that political power exists on many different layers and that our traditional view of the role of the state has to change. From this we can conclude either that the state is limited in its powers or that the state has a wider influence through its many alliances and through joint intervention on global issues. Whichever we choose, we have to admit that the power of the state is more diffused than it has been. We are living in a period in which the role of the state is being transformed. Politics can never be the same.

Another important issue to consider is the rise of the INGO. Many people belong to such organizations to show their concern for environmental, gender or peace issues, among others. These also are becoming global in scope and in influence. For many people in these organizations, collaboration between governments is not enough. The decision-making process needs to be influenced from outside. Strategies for exercising such influence range from working with government to attacking the government.

The number of such organizations is growing all the time. In 1909 there were thirty-seven IGOs and 176 INGOs. In 1996 there were nearly 260 IGOs and 5472 INGOs. There has been an explosion in these kinds of operation and in the forms of diplomacy that go with them. IGOs have to cover everything from agreements on whaling to policing the use of airspace.

INGOs often exercise their power not only in the attempt to achieve their goals but also in order to counterbalance powerful vested interests which they perceive to be acting in a destructive way. Lord Peter Melchett, the Chairman of Greenpeace, in an interview for *Third Way* magazine, talked about ICI, which was lobbying the government to lift the ban on hydroflurocarbon (HFC) emissions. Greenpeace felt a responsibility to balance that campaign. Lord Melchett saw that power was shifting to the corporations, and said that if Greenpeace was to change things it had to 'follow the power' – a telling phrase. He continued:

> Any of our campaigns in the 70s and 80s would have targeted the political process – through international conventions to protect Antarctica, for example, or to ban nuclear testing, even to stop the dumping of nuclear waste or burning of toxic waste in the North Sea. You'd get Denmark to ban incineration in the hope that Sweden would, and then the Germans and the Dutch and, eventually, the French and the British would be forced to, and that's how it worked. A lot of our campaigns now are more likely trying to get Safeway and Tesco to ban GM food – or to get Nike to say that it won't use PVC, in the hope that eventually the European Union will see that PVC is on its way out. Coca-Cola has just said that its going to stop using HFCs and you hope that will make the government see that HFCs don't have a future.[9]

This highlights the trend for the balance of power to shift from the state to the corporation. If you want to effect change, target the corporation. This shift in power to big business is one of the first things people think about when they consider the nature of globalization.

In his first speech on the environment, delivered in October 2000, Prime Minister Tony Blair called for a coalition 'which stretches across national frontiers' between government, corporations and INGOs to address environmental issues in an effective way. The role of government was, he said, to create a framework within which business could operate. So tax benefits and other rewards would be conferred on those businesses that became greener in their practices. Rejecting the 'myth of the wicked multinational', he called businesses to realize that there were profits to be made out of green products and services in a growing market worth $335 billion, which is as large as the world market for pharmaceuticals or aerospace. He placed this new coalition in the context of the Kyoto Protocol, the International Agreement on Environmental Strategy and European environmental standards.

Here are all the components of global politics. Environmental issues, which defy the confines of political authority, have become urgent. Attention has been drawn to them by pressure groups, scientists and the media. The government response is one element among others, including a global agreement (Kyoto), a regional context (European standards), the need for transboundary co-operation, the recognition that action must mean coalition, and the acknowledgment that power belongs to the corporations, which will act effectively only if there are positive incentives to do so. We, the citizens, are addressed primarily as consumers who wish to buy green products, but also as people who wish to create a better world for our children. The government sets up commissions, invests money in schemes for alternative energy and adjusts its transport policy so that it becomes greener. Yet amid a plethora of new initiatives, Tony Blair's speech, which was positive and optimistic, admitted that governments can do little in the face of such a global challenge without forming alliances. Yet despite this urgency national interests can still dominate the agenda. Within weeks of assuming the presidency of the United States of America, George Bush placed America's need for more fuel above its commitment to concerted action against environmental degradation.

So, is the state more limited in its power? It is certainly the case that no one multinational has *more* power than the state. Neither has any one INGO. In the face of such issues, all players have to act together in order to bring about change. They all have to admit to compromise. Yet each government wants results in order to fly its own flag. The identity of the nation has not been swamped.

Nevertheless, within this coalition the power has transferred from the state to the corporation. Within the traditional boundaries of the nation, in so far as they can still be defined, the state still seems to have power, and certainly has the consent of its people. But outside, in the world of transboundary problems, power is shared and increasingly resides elsewhere. Governments are busier than they have ever been, addressing more agendas, meeting internationally and, together with the legislature, building a body of international law to cope with global demands. The long, international debate over the trial of General Pinochet was a good example of the way the profile of international law, international courts of justice and human-rights legislation was raised. Similarly, in the latter part of the twentieth century, nation-states worked together in going to war in the Gulf and the Balkans. These examples illustrate the extent of the transformation we are witnessing. The state is not being obliterated, but it is being limited. The question is, 'Can democracy work beyond borders?'

The impact of corporate power

In the twenty-first century, then, it seems we may be governed by business rather than by politics. Certainly, we live in a world where many markets are dominated by a few very large companies. In 1998 there were 53,000 multinationals with 450,000 foreign subsidiaries. They had global sales of $9.5 trillion. They accounted for almost 65% of world trade, and for about 80% of world trade in technology. The hundred largest multinationals control about 20% of all global foreign assets, employ six million workers and account for almost 30% of the total worldwide sales of all multinationals. Yet while this situation has been developing, small and medium-sized companies have also been expanding rapidly. The liberalization of trade and communications is helping them also to be integrated into global markets.

The late twentieth century saw many mergers and acquisitions, with large companies emerging from the privatization of previously nationalized industries in the UK. In the US, Microsoft grew so huge that its monopoly power adversely affected the fastest-growing industry in the world. All this has led many people to feel that because corporations are not democratically accountable in the same way as governments, nothing can be done to curtail their influence, which, it is assumed, will be bad.

This underestimates two facts: first, the influence of consumer power on the corporation. Not only can consumers protest by boycotting a company's products or selling its shares, but consumer groups and pressure groups can have a marked impact on its behaviour. People are more likely to join such agencies than they are to vote in elections – an additional sign that people feel that the locus of power in the global economy is shifting. According to think-tank Demos,

> A recent survey of representative samples in twenty-five countries found that social responsibility was the most influential factor in public impressions of individual companies, and one in five consumers reported actively rewarding or punishing a company for its perceived social performance.[10]

The impact of the Jubilee 2000 campaign, which called for the cancellation of developing countries' debts to the West, indicates that there are issues on which INGOs can effectively challenge the behaviour of both governments and banks. Such movements can only become more important as truly global ways of operating become essential.

The second fact is the speed at which innovation takes place in the information economy. Large multinationals can sometimes be slower to innovate than smaller, more focused companies. In the old heavy-industrial economy the large took over the small. In the new weightless economy the fast overtake the slow. Multinationals therefore have to look over their shoulder all the time. There are few long-term profits to be had in a technological society where, as soon as an innovative product is successful, it is copied by competitors. In a high-tech economy, speed is of the essence, since time is the new scarce resource.

If corporate power is in the ascendancy, the market will continue to grow; but an important question is: what happens to the people over whom it has most power? People have value, not because they are a 'resource', but because they have intrinsic high worth. Why are people who are of equal worth left out of this equation to live in poverty?

The behaviour of multinationals is particularly problematic in the developing world. One example was highlighted by the BBC documentary programme *Panorama*,[11] which claimed that despite having ethical policies about conditions for their workforce in Asia, Nike and Gap infringed basic rights by employing child labour, or by requiring their workers to work longer hours than stipulated. The programme prompted an immediate reaction from the companies involved. Both had elaborate codes of conduct which, they claimed, were rigorously enforced. Yet they also admitted that by sourcing materials in the Third World problems could arise. Both were extremely sensitive to public opinion, showing that in a globalized world with an international investigative media the accusation of behaving unethically is one that corporations wish to avoid.

In China, despite economic growth, most people make less than $1 per day and, in most factories where toys are made, trade unions are not allowed. According to the United Nations Development Programme, in 1996 the combined assets of the world's 358 billionaires exceeded the combined income of 45% of the world's population. It is no wonder that James Wolfensohn, President of the World Bank, has said of the working of financial markets that 'at the level of people, the system isn't working'.

The importance of this issue cannot be overestimated. If all citizens are to enjoy the benefits of membership of the global community, there will have to be a much higher commitment to corporate responsibility worldwide, and much greater extension of human and labour rights to those countries that do not provide them. Sadly, there is no mechanism by which this can be enforced. Media exposure or campaigns by INGOs are important inputs into this process. Multinationals must realize that consumers are becoming increasingly ethical and more sophisticated in their spending and investment. In the pursuit of greater transparency, many leading multinationals have responded to this climate by introducing social and environmental audits alongside conventional financial audits. For them, democracy means working not only within international law but also according to ethical practice, honesty, transparency and environmental sustainability. Even though they are not democratically accountable, by doing these things they hope to be given 'proxy consent' by consumers, NGOs and governments, who see them as an ally and not a threat to democratic accountability and the goals of civil society.

Some poorer countries have grown economically in recent years. The Institute for Development Studies points out that living standards grew in East Asia after the 1960s and in China and India particularly after 1980. The Chinese economy grew at an annual rate of 10.2% during the 1980s and 12.8% during the first half of the 1990s. But who is receiving this money? In many countries there is still gross inequality in living standards, and, as mentioned above, the gap is widening between rich and poor throughout the world, including within countries such as China. While the rich throughout the world are benefiting from the greater freedom to trade, there is little impetus to protect the poor by meeting their most basic requirements. Moreover, focusing on the poorest of the poor may lead us to forget the broad working class throughout the world who make only a precarious living.

If the world economy grows at the expense of the poor, it needs to be managed in a better way. Yet at the moment there are no global institutions with the power to bring about that process. The International Monetary Fund exists to bail out countries in short-term debt. It tends to be dominated by the United States. It carries no weight among the developing nations, many of which are hostile to the way it treats countries when offering loans. Its austerity measures are famous for their impact on already poor societies.

Others look to the United Nations for global governance, and, with its model of inclusion, there is much to be said for exploring this avenue. The problem is that the United Nations has little authority to act, partly because it is so inclusive and has such a wide membership. It is a supreme example of a forum where bartering takes place and deals are made. But it has no authority in the world of global financial markets. Because there is no one institution which can act effectively in all the areas where globalization requires us to act, we are currently following a model of international collaboration.

The church's response

In today's 'multi-layered government', politics operates on the local, national, regional and international levels. The question this poses is whether we are willing to become 'multiple citizens', seeing ourselves as having responsibilities on each of those levels. Many already do so. Voting conscientiously and supporting world aid, they are aware of the needs of the world and their place in it. We are called to become cosmopolitan in ethos.

It is sometimes difficult to see the relevance of the faith of the church to such issues. Some dismiss discussions such as these as technical or even as lacking in Christian content. But in fact there is a profound challenge to our Christian faith here. In the Introduction, we considered the four voices of the church. Each is important as a response to globalization. First, the church is called to responsibility; it is to stand for the maintenance of all those institutions and commitments that ensure dignity, freedom and peace for people throughout the world. We are to work lest the powers that have been unleashed should destroy the environment of which we are trustees, or weaken good governance.

Secondly, the church is called to celebrate the world in all its diversity and to maintain the best of all cultures, their wisdom, their arts and in fact everything that represents each culture's identity. It is impossible to celebrate a bland, commercial anti-culture that travels with western products and tends to obliterate indigenous culture.

But there is more than this. We are, thirdly, called to offer resistance. The Jubilee 2000 campaign on Third World debt is a good example of this, although many campaigns against world poverty and the abuse of human rights also illustrate the point. Of course, many other individuals and groups, not motivated by any faith, also protest against injustice. But the church is called to do so because God is a God of justice who cares for all those who are oppressed. Oppression is not just about poverty. It is also about moral poverty in an amoral society. The church does not make itself popular when it speaks out in this area, but it is the voice of prophecy, the voice of resistance.

Lastly, we cannot be triumphalistic in a world which has so many suffering people in it. The church is called to suffer with those who suffer, and to alleviate that suffering, whether through medical or other aid, human-rights work or comfort for the distressed. Though risen from the dead, Christ still bears the marks of the crucifixion, and we must honour his identification with all who suffer as well as being willing to suffer ourselves if necessary. If the process of globalization increases poverty (for instance, if we in the North cause environmental degradation in the South through over-consumption), the church suffers with those who suffer and offers help to reverse the situation if possible.

Globalization is meant to be a product of the modern world's success. Yet within the export of our achievements and the demonstration of our prowess there is a hollow culture. The heart of a culture is a commitment to truth, without which it has little to offer. But we have put truth on trial ...

3
Truth on trial

At the very least, we have to face up to whether we are happy with the impact globalization is having on our own society. Of course, there are enormous benefits. Western countries enjoy a mixed culture which is much richer and deeper than it was because of the presence of people from all over the world. But are we concerned that the concept of citizenship is so weak in our society? It is important to see ourselves as 'multiple citizens' in a global order, but, if we have lost any idea of what it means to be a citizen, we are in real difficulty as a community. We need to recover the local. There are many ways in which we can lose our sense of local identity, and throughout the world there is a movement to re-establish expressions of cultural identity.

Global and local

At present, globalization is not about making a universal culture but about mixing cultures. It is not about converging to a fixed point; indeed, it is essential to an understanding of globalization that we are all going to remain different to some extent. Of course, the process is dominated by those who are most prominent in the market-place, since it is through the market that globalization occurs most effectively. This means that American culture, in particular, is pervasive in its impact. American technology, goods, movies, TV and political influence are to be found throughout the world.

Globalization has many ways of affecting the situation within a country. Economist John Gray uses the phrase 'de-localization' to describe one of them. Commercial activities lose their local identity as products that are not locally sourced are marketed using western images. Local knowledge is bypassed as multinationals sell across cultural boundaries.

This threat to local identity is also apparent in the way that the demand for local cultural identity is re-establishing itself. In many countries, the nation was composed of different ethnic groups held together by some sense of shared identity legitimated by the authority of the state. The boundaries of the state may not have mirrored the territorial claims of those groups, but since identity was shared there seemed to be no problem. But in some areas of the world the politics of identity is re-emerging as a focus for political life. Ethnic groups are establishing old boundaries. Local identities are becoming more important to us. Regional government has become an issue once again.

The attempt to re-localize is a response to de-localization. Sometimes this is worked out by peaceful means such as devolution, as in Scotland and Wales. Sometimes ethnic languages which have fallen into disuse are revived. But some countries have been torn apart as old ethnic rivalries have re-emerged. Ethnic conflicts in the former Yugoslavia are a recent tragic example. As globalization proceeds and identities are changed by exposure to values from outside, people attempt to go back to their roots and find sources of an identity that may have a better chance of survival than the one artificially imposed on them by historical accident, colonial possession or the outcome of warfare.

Identity is usually guarded by tradition, the means by which both wisdom and folly are passed down from one generation to another. Globalization can be seen as an attack on the deepest traditions of the culture. Attacking a nation's tradition can be as much of a threat as attacking its land.

The process of globalization conveys a powerful ethical message: though cultures may be different, none has any right to call itself superior. If no culture is superior, no god is superior. We are called to respect all cultures equally. On the face of it, this would seem to make for greater harmony. It could, for instance, bring about an 'ecumenical' world in which commitment to cultural equality enables us to accept our differences. But not all societies are willing to lay down their strongly held convictions to facilitate a form of tolerance that they may see as distinctively western.

Islamic societies are struggling with this facet of globalization. How do they retain their religious and cultural distinctiveness while enjoying the benefits of a global society? Some have solved this problem by opting out of modernity, as in Afghanistan, where the Taleban rule a newly medievalized culture. But the problem will not go away. Islamic societies may have strict laws about the way women may be portrayed or the way they should dress in public, but satellite television and the internet give easy access to western images that threaten to undermine the values of those cultures. As western cultural preferences become universally accessible, local cultural practices increasingly tend to be compared with them. Islamic views on women, for instance, may be defended by comparison with western concepts of human rights or liberal ideas about the role of women in society. Such a process will, in some cases, be fiercely resisted as a society that claims that its values are based on divine revelation finds itself under threat from a western culture perceived to be decadent. The West and Islam have a tendency to Satanize each other, thus getting a distorted picture of the other's culture. The idea that no culture is superior is at the heart of globalization, and it also enables those who dominate the markets to place profits before respect. Moreover, they assume that because they are economically dominant they are *ipso facto* superior.

The place of tradition

The West is a post-traditional culture. It is not that traditions are absent, but that the function and place of tradition have changed. In a traditional society, such as a pre-modern one, many aspects of life are accepted as given. One's place in life, occupation or marriage partner may not be a matter for individual choice. In western society, the fact that tradition expresses the wisdom of previous generations does not mean that it is automatically accepted. It is another option among many. One can choose to be traditional. As Professor Anthony Giddens writes:

> Tradition more and more must be contemplated, defended, sifted through, in relation to the awareness that there exists a variety of other ways of doing things. ... Individuals have to

decide today not only when and whom to marry, but whether to marry at all. 'Having a child' need not any longer have anything to do with marriage, and is a precious and difficult decision for both men and women, far from the circumstances of the past when such a thing, in many situations, seemed more or less natural. One even has to settle what one's sexuality is as well as grasp what relationships are and how they might best be constructed.[1]

We see the proliferation of choice as a key feature of freedom in our society. But choice may not bring freedom. It may bring anxiety and insecurity about the wisdom of the choices one has made. Tradition is not a refuge from choice; it has become a choice itself. It has lost its in-built authority either as the wisdom of previous generations or as the repository of divine revelation. In a fast-changing world we see freedom of choice as more important than tradition, and the future as more important than the past. Since no culture can claim to be superior, any worldview that claims to be a standard by which others are judged must be cut down to size.

The Christian tradition, with its attendant ethical perspectives, has become one of these options. Yet the idea that all worldviews are equal is itself a position which, on its own premises, is not superior to other viewpoints and cannot claim to judge them. Consequently, either one must admit that, since no ethical values can be said to be superior, there is no possibility of reasonable debate; or one must regard one view as superior – in this case, the view that no view is superior! It is this second option that is prevalent in modern discourse albeit one that is hidden. Christian thinking may be vigorously attacked because it claims to be true, yet those who attack it deny that their position makes a similar claim to truth.

The relativism at the heart of postmodern worldviews ironically denies authority in its traditional form of 'power over' others. This loss of authority has led to two different reactions. One is the despair inherent in some forms of postmodernism; the other is the rise of fundamentalism.

Despair and the breakdown of institutions

Back in the 1960s and 1970s, many sociologists suggested that institutions were breaking down. For many of them this was a good thing, as they were seen to wield inappropriate power. There is no doubt that trust in institutions once unquestioningly thought to be right and good is breaking down. In the new millennium, the statistics seem to speak for themselves. In Britain, two out of five marriages ends in divorce. Only one child in two is expected to spend its entire childhood living with its married, natural parents.[2]

Politics too has suffered. In a poll commissioned for Channel 4 television, 30% of the respondents went as far as to say that Britain is not a democracy, and 71% agreed with the statement that 'the voting system produces governments that do not represent the views of most ordinary people'.[3] In a survey of young people's attitudes commissioned by Barnardos it was found that 27% of those questioned had no interest at all in politics, and only 21% of the sample claimed to 'support' a political party. This led to the conclusion that a third of the adult population-to-be is uninterested in politics.[4] In the 2001 General Election more people stayed at home than went out to vote.

Then there is the 'breakdown of the church'. In 1900, 30% of the adult population were church members; in 1995 it was 13.9%.[5] When George Carey, the Archbishop of Canterbury, called for a revolution in morality to save the country from crime and degradation, some television programmes and newspaper articles said he had no right to suggest we are immoral.[6]

The secularization thesis argued that religious institutions, actions and consciousness had lost their social significance. But the relationship between religious institutions and society is not that simple. For instance, sociologist Grace Davies maintains that while religious belief is strong in Britain, people who hold those beliefs do not belong to a church. While religion is influential, its institutions are not.[7]

Peter Berger claimed that secularization was really religion bearing its own consequences. The criterion by which people decided what to believe was now personal preference rather than a concept of the revealed truth, and this he termed the 'heretical imperative'. But Berger also prophesied that one day humanity would move back into a system of institutions. The lack of trust in institutions was temporary. Humanity cherished order too much for it to be otherwise.[8] Berger saw this cultural revolution in very negative terms. Postmodernists themselves can see the problems that accompany lack of order. Choice is fine, but chaos is not. I am reminded of those Old Testament words, 'In those days Israel had no king; everyone did as he saw fit.'[9]

The rise of fundamentalism

Fundamentalism is a defence against pluralism. Pluralism requires truth claims to be open to dialogue. Fundamentalism, by contrast, asserts truth with a degree of certainty that is not open to question. It refuses to say, 'I may be wrong.' It links faith with certainty, and is seen as a threat because there is no possibility of deflecting people from what may be false and dangerous beliefs by reasoned argument. Fundamentalism is a response to the globalization of pluralist values. What is remarkable about fundamentalism is not the fact that it defends tradition but the manner in which it defends it. It poses a challenge to the idea of a truly global and cosmospolitan world. At its heart is a refusal to dialogue.

Why do we fear fundamentalism? Partly because the refusal to dialogue and the possibility of violence appear to go together. One need only look at the history of Northern Ireland to see this. In many places, particularly in Islamic theocracies, religious fundamentalism is mixed with strong nationalism and maybe political dictatorship. We fear those as well. We fear anything that looks different from the freedom of democracy. Maybe we fear religious fundamentalism because it is presented to us in very stark pictures of people behaving differently from our norms. Islamic fundamentalists appear as women clothed in black from head to toe, or as crowds of men beating themselves into a frenzy in public displays of devotion, as in the Haj. Islam's claim to be a peaceful religion is lost in media images of militant Muslims, although they are a minority within Islam.

But there is something more. We fear fundamentalism because it suggests that other people can live without doubt. Perhaps we conclude that they are brain-washed or being dictated to. Or perhaps the problem lies with us. Fundamentalism's heightened level of certainty challenges postmodernity. We know that the world is not that certain, but how pleasant it would be if it were! Are the benefits of doubt and dialogue really worth the effort? It would be a lot easier to give in and to be told what to believe by some higher authority.

We may fear that our liberalism is not doing our world any favours. In an article entitled 'Killing for God', *Time* magazine commented:

> ... wherever the word of God is cherished, it now seems some clutch of believers is becoming more certain that faith compels a resort to violent measures ... At bottom, what the desperadoes who kill in God's name seem to share is an uneasy sense that secularism and the principles of tolerance in democracy – which often require a shade less certainty in one's own beliefs – have left religion a weak brew. [10]

Fundamentalism will not go away. Indeed, it will be an important part of the map of the twenty-first century, and it is therefore vital that we understand it. It can influence political agendas, as was seen in the Iranian revolution of 1979. Sometimes it takes the form of cults that can end in tragedy, as in the mass suicide of the Branch Davidians led by David Koresh in Waco, Texas.

Fundamentalism is conservative in its worldview. It defends a world in which issues are black and white, as opposed to the ambiguities of conventional religion. It often subscribes to a literalist view of its scriptures, interpreting them in a way that would not be recognizable to the rest of the faithful. It may be used to promote other cultural commitments that may be racist, sexist or otherwise oppressive. (For instance, the Iranian revolution may have been due, in part, to the threat of modernization and globalization to the vested interests of the clerics and the merchants of that country.) Sometimes it propounds doctrines that have only a tenuous connection with traditional religious teaching, or which are even a pernicious distortion of it, as in the 'health and wealth' movement in Christianity, which teaches that both those goods characterize the successful Christian life.

Fundamentalism is more than conservatism. It is a defensive state of mind, which, because it divides the world into 'us' and 'them', is always prone to being reactionary and aggressive. It has an ambiguous relationship with modernity. On the one hand, it sees it as undermining the truth. On the other hand, it may use modern technology and set up huge, expensive organizations to further its cause. Some evangelists in America are well known for their television broadcasting, and the use of the internet in religious mission is increasing rapidly. Yet despite large audiences, there is no dialogue about the message or its veracity – only an invitation to convert or to become otherwise involved in the work.

The irony is that liberals can be every bit as fixed in their mindset as fundamentalists. They also can be selective in their use of Scripture and just as forceful in applying it. They can see fundamentalists under every bed and overreact when caution is advisable.[11] Theologian John Macquarrie asked:

> What is meant by 'liberal' theology? If it means only that the theologian to whom the adjective is applied has an openness to other points of view, then liberal theologians are found in all schools of thought. But if 'liberal' becomes itself a party label, then it usually turns out to be extremely illiberal.[12]

After all, in a post-traditional world there is nothing wrong in holding to the traditions of the past and in defending the veracity of the Scriptures, the sanctity of marriage and the importance of Christian ethics. Yet there is an increasing tendency to use the word 'fundamentalist' of any who hold to traditional Christian beliefs. An alternative is to refer to them as 'right-wing'. Presumably the latter is an attempt to put all those with such views into the box marked 'Moral Majority' – a term that has become synonymous with right-wing pressure groups in the United States. This use of labels that are unacceptable in a liberal secular society seems intended to provoke people with whom one disagrees. The majority of people who hold traditional views, however, are not fundamentalists in the defensive sense referred to above, but Christians worshipping within the mainstream denominations, or Muslims living peacefully in a plural society, who see no need to change their religious convictions just because the culture has changed around them.

While we do well to be apprehensive of the growth of fundamentalism, therefore, we also need to regard it as a complex problem. It is one thing for fundamentalists to place themselves outside community relationships by becoming sectarian. But if we make no attempt to engage in dialogue with them, or refuse to do so, the world will become a more dangerous place. Tolerance without engagement is indifference. Real tolerance involves community. If we are to overcome our fear of those we disagree with the most, and of their views, we must form relationships with them. Those relationships must be characterized by respect if conversation is to take place at all.

Without belief in tradition to guide us as a society, we are exposed to all kinds of vested interests, media messages and fashions. It is easy to be blown from one notion to another. On the one hand, a vacuous openness may produce despair; on the other, defensive fundamentalism may threaten open dialogue. Although tradition could sometimes be manipulated to oppress, it always provided a way of seeing the world that emphasized continuity between the generations and helped to foster a sense of rootedness. It is within the Christian tradition of 2,000 years that this is most marked. Within the context of church worship, hymns are sung that were penned 500 years ago, and prayers are read that were written out of the experience of the Reformation. They still express the beliefs of modern Christians. Theology is built on the foundation of those who lived at the time of Christ or in the earliest centuries of Hebrew thought. Here is a tradition that is constantly renewing itself because it claims to contain an inviolate truth. Some things are true whether we believe them to be so or not.

Truth and power

Postmodernism has a rather different approach to truth. In typically postmodern manner Jean-François Lyotard defined postmodernity as 'incredulity towards metanarratives'.[13] In other words it mistrusts Big Stories or all-encompassing explanations of life, such as Christianity, Islam or Marxism. Nevertheless, what is postmodernity as a description of a cultural epoch, if not precisely an all-encompassing explanation? It ends up shooting itself in the foot. If postmodernity is all about images, why do academics write books to express their ideas about it? If there are no authorities left, why do they constantly quote Lyotard, Derrida and Baudrillard? The postmodernists respond that this is precisely the point of postmodernity: it is contradiction, parody and irony. You can't win. Trying to define or analyse postmodernity flies in the face of the way it wants us to view the world.

Most of us do not live with a totally postmodern worldview. It would be hard to do so in a world that is still predominantly set up for 'modern', reason-based life. But, equally, most of us no longer live with a totally modern worldview. Postmodernity has influenced us, and so have worldviews that are neither western nor Christian. At the very time that western values are spreading all over the world, the idea that these values represent universal truths is being denied. In a postmodern world, truth is not universal, but local. When Lyotard talked of the end of metanarratives, he saw them as local stories that had got blown out of all proportion. Presumably Christianity should have stayed near Galilee. It is also the case, he said, that the more local a story is, the truer it is likely to be. Since the context is part of the truth, the more we generalize the more we neglect the context. Therefore anybody who claims to tell the truth about the meaning of life is wrong by definition.

Within postmodernity, scepticism about truth is not confined to the religious realm. Science also is under fire. Science has been the testing-ground for the idea that rationalism can give us the tools to control nature. In a postmodern world, scientific truth is not objective truth, but just another set of beliefs. After all, it has not delivered the world it said it would. Acid rain, nuclear bombs and pollution are the heritage of modern scientific claims to truth. Why should we believe them any more?

For the postmodernists, those Big Stories that have survived have done so because they were more powerful than true. Indeed, all truth claims are disguises for power. The elevation of rationalism as a universal value was peculiar to western cultures. The prominence of the ideas of the European Enlightenment in the world is due not to their truth but to the degree of power they wielded. From this perspective Christianity is pervasive, not because it is true but because it travelled the world on the back of colonization.

In arguing that theological truth is local, contextual and plural rather than objective and universal, theologian Walter Brueggemann says:

> We are now able to see that what has passed for objective universal knowledge has in fact been the interested claim of the dominant voices who were able to pose their view and to gain either assent or docile acceptance from those whose interest the claim did not serve. Objectivity is in fact one more practice of ideology that presents interest in covert form as established fact.[14]

His statement is a very good summary of the implication of postmodernity for theology. He also says:

> It is clear on many fronts, not only in theology but in very many disciplines, that the old modes of knowing that are Euro-American, male and white, no longer command respect and credibility as objective and universally true. Indeed older modes of assertion about reality have an increasingly empty ring, even if we do not understand all the reasons for the change.[15]

We are to listen, then, to the voices from the margins. Mainstream claims to truth may reflect bids for power; listen instead to those who are oppressed. Of course, we must be wise. They also may have their agendas and make bids for power, but if we listen only to mainstream voices our perspective is prejudiced from the start. In a postmodern culture all worldviews are equal; nobody has any right to claim superiority. Each person has the right to tell his or her own story, and Christians have this right like everybody else. But it is heard only as a story, not as a witness to objective truth. In a postmodern culture, the freedom we undeniably have to tell our own personal story of faith is won at a high cost: the denial of the transcendence of God. To claim that my personal story is a version of *the* story is seen as offensive.

Postmodernity can be seen as a descent into despair. There are no trustworthy explanations of who or what we are. We are members of an age of lost innocence. David Bosch has said:

> This hostility towards reason, which seems indeed to suggest that any form of human dialogue and mutual intelligibility is unattainable, cannot but lead to a total breakdown in inter-human communication and ultimately to chaos.[16]

I cannot say that something is true for you. If I do, I am taking power over you. This is oppressive, and undermines what you are saying. Suspicion of truth claims is everywhere. The charismatic may claim to have witnessed physical healing in a public meeting where others see manipulation and the exploitation of the weak. I may claim to have a better argument than you, but others hear rhetoric and my attempt to coerce you to conform to my values. I may claim that the Bible is the Word of God, while others view this as delusion since, in their view, no one reading of any text is authoritative.

This means that we have to look hard at how our claims to know truth come over. Our society believes that exercising our freedom of choice will enable us to choose whatever constitutes truth for us. But the Christian view of the relationship between truth and freedom is the opposite. We do not find truth through freedom of choice. God reveals it to us. For this reason Lesslie Newbigin has said that 'truth is not the fruit of freedom, it is the precondition of freedom'.[17] Jesus said 'You will know the truth, and the truth will set you free.'[18] We become free when we are enabled to live lives based on the truth. This is true not only for individuals but also in relationships and for entire societies. We do not have to search for truth, but rather to recognize it and to build our lives on it.

This approach is not the road to fundamentalism, as some may fear. Believing that something is true does not mean that I should be a dogmatist. It means that I should attempt to persuade people of its truth, but in doing so respect their own belief or unbelief. Not to respect them in this way is to hold a sub-Christian view of them, and turns my attempt to persuade them of truth into manipulation. I cannot, as a Christian, stop being involved in mission. To claim that I have found God in Christ compels me to share that news with others. To fail to do so contradicts my claim. But in doing so I must remember that listening conveys love; it also brings understanding. Jesus said to his disciples that the kings of the Gentiles lorded over them, but that his disciples were not to act in that way. The one who rules should be like the one who serves. 'For who is greater, the one who is at the table or the one who serves? Is it not the one who is at the table? But I am among you as one who serves.'[19]

If those outside the Christian church are to be convinced of the truth of the Christian faith, the suspicion at the heart of postmodernity will have to be allayed. The tension between truth and power is at the heart of that process. It is not just that our works must back up our words. That is always the case. But in the postmodern era suspicion can be allayed only by trust, which means building long-term and open relationships with those who are not Christians. The issue of power can be dealt with only when Christianity becomes the servant of the world rather than its empire-builder.

Consumption and meaning

In the postmodern world, consumption is one of the visible anchors of identity. It is hard to live with nihilism, or at least hard to live rationally with it. The consequences of the decision to do so are stark and uncompromising. Consumerism is a way of avoiding that emptiness. Our society finds itself needing a distraction, and consumerism is a convenient consolation. It consoles us for the death of God and for the restlessness that that loss has brought about. Whether the goods we buy are important or not is difficult to say. Some, of course, are the necessities of life: food, clothing and shelter. But the consumer culture we live in has attached moral, aesthetic and even spiritual values to the goods we purchase, so that the act of consumption feels in some sense a worthy one. It is this pursuit of values that shows that consumerism is in fact a masquerade. G. K. Chesterton once said that every man who ever knocked on the door of a brothel was looking for God. In our age the brothel has become the shopping mall.

When Jesus said that it was impossible to serve both God and

Money, he described them both as masters. Both make demands on the individual soul. They seek to occupy the same space in the human heart, but they are mutually exclusive.

Consumption is not just consolation, it is also symbolism. We attach not just values to goods but also the symbols and rituals that once belonged to religious life. Consumer goods convey messages about those who buy them because they are attached to the symbolic worldview portrayed in the advertising and marketing that surround them. They may be symbols of power or prestige, sexual virility, femininity or masculinity. We are invited to believe that we can become what we consume. Such a society demonstrates, yet again, how empty the soul is. It is as if we now believe that accumulation is a worthy replacement for spiritual growth. Jesus asks us to choose between two modes of human existence. One is marked by spiritual restlessness for more of God, the other by material restlessness for more of anything but God.

The mistake we often make is to think that because these two are mutually exclusive, they are entirely different from one another. But in fact the opposite is the case. They are two sides of the same coin. The problem is that they are so similar in their aims. Accusing western society of materialism, which on the evidence is a perfectly reasonable thing to do, can set the church off on a mistaken interpretation of that evidence. It is the search for something of ultimate significance that is important. People want to feel good and look good. They want to have an adventure, a positive experience of the world. They may shop for a 'new look' because they need affirmation, or lose themselves in the paraphernalia of hobbies or computer hardware to 'give them an interest'. But all this is rarely done to excess. For most people it is 'little and often'. Many visits to the shopping mall result in no purchases at all. Young people, couples and families wander around looking at the goods, drinking the coffee and being part of a consumer experience. Surrounded by so many choices, they feel as if they have found what they were looking for, and leave. In his book *Ego and Soul*, Australian sociologist John Carroll says:

> Gratified desire, the goal of so much of human endeavour, is tantalisingly elusive: the formative childhood image of it

comes from the mood in which fairy-tales end. However, there are moments in which every individual achieves that longed-for state, and those moments cast some of the lines of hope that govern life through the in-betweens, and pattern the way he will at once compromise his deepest desires and console himself for the discontent that the compromises cause him. Consumption has taken over from religious ritual as the main source of compromise and consolation.[20]

Yet though shopping malls are now designed around offering us an experience, their sole purpose is to sell us goods. To keep the wheels of the market turning, we are told of risks, dangers and inadequacies that beset us, and of products we can buy that will help. Mere wants are turned into vital needs: we *must* have a certain product. Economic growth, portrayed as so desirable, turns out to be fuelled by discontent. The Christian virtue of contentment stops this aspect of our culture dead in its tracks.

But is the consumer culture just that, or has it become a culture of addiction? Mark Stibbe comments:

The truth of the matter is that we are all doing something, every day, to drive off the boredom, to mask the pain, and to take a holiday from reality. Some of us are more dependent on certain things than others. But we are all addicts, and we are all of us part of an addictive culture.[21]

Many people are not addicted to shopping or to the philosophy of consumerism. To make such a claim that would be to go too far. But addiction *is* one of the hallmarks of our society. All addicts need *more* of whatever they are hooked on in order to satisfy them. An interesting aspect of consumer culture is the gap opening up between our standard of living and our quality of life. In most working households, both partners have jobs and have to fit other areas of life around them. More than one marriage in three breaks down, and single-adult households are increasing as a result. Our communities are fragmenting. Stress-related illness is on the increase. Part of the stress people feel is a sense of powerlessness. They are hemmed in both by the demands of their employers and also by the demands they make on themselves in pursuit of their desired standard of living. So their quality of life suffers.

One of the traps in which our addiction ensnares us is personal debt. In the past, saving was a sign of personal integrity. Frugality and thrift were hallmarks of a responsible attitude to life. Engaged couples would 'save up to get married'. Patience was a virtue. Consumer durables were not so essential that one went into debt in order to have them. There was pride in owning as well as in possessing, and it was important not to be indebted to anybody. Bankruptcy was a matter of shame.

In contemporary society we have precisely the opposite phenomenon. We have allowed our moral values to become so distorted that what was formerly bad is now considered good. The term 'credit' is applied to what our grandparents called 'debt'. The connotations of credit are nearly all positive. Multiple credit cards demonstrate not indebtedness but creditworthiness. Saving is still good, of course, but why save for what you can have now? As one famous advert put it, 'Access takes the waiting out of wanting.' If you reach your credit limit you will be offered a higher one. To have more is to be more. But the addiction to having without owning leads people into a trap from which they find it difficult to escape. Somebody, somewhere, is profiting from their addiction.

Addicts abuse drugs or alcohol as a means to an end. They are looking to numb the pain, get a buzz or find peace. John Carroll talks of consumption in the same way:

> There may be moments when a new pair of shoes or a standard lamp so catch the purchaser's fancy that she does feel that the Gods have blessed her with one of their finest gifts. But she has been deluded. Genuine gifts transfigure the person and her human relations. They announce new possibilities, as the angel Gabriel of Renaissance art announced to the Virgin Mary the miracle that would change her destiny. They are memorable. Consumption does not have any of these qualities. The most it can satisfy is a satellite wish that moves in the reflected light of its sun.[22]

How can we sum up the mood of our society at the start of the new millennium? At the very least, it does not seem very optimistic. It regards the modern, Enlightenment world as passing away. That worldview promised much and delivered a great deal, but the game is up and it is time to move on. Modernity's universal claims are now suspect. Other worldviews are rising that have a very different philosophical background. This has led to the suspicion, that far from being universal truths, Enlightenment claims were in fact disguises for power, in the form of colonialism, the oppression of women and of ethnic groups, and other forms of injustice. The application of reason based on scepticism has led to its own demise, and to a fragmented, listless society, that is uncertain about its own future. The Enlightenment appears now to have fostered a misplaced faith in humanity – a race that has turned out to be capable of evils that modernist optimism neither anticipated nor could explain.

There is therefore no further room for belief in big ideologies. They have comprehensively let us down. All that is left is consumerism. There is no 'being' left in being human; there is only the pleasure of having. There is no future in intellectual enquiry, not only because there is no agreed basis for it, but also because it has let us down. There is only the distraction of the entertainment culture – of surface rather than depth, and of hedonism. We do not care for history because we are rootless, drifting through life from one experience to another, and one consumption opportunity to another. History itself has been packaged as a commodity; museums and heritage sites are now leisure places, marketed to attract the attention of distracted people.

Yet could this listlessness be a sign of spiritual life? Literary critic Susan Sontag writes:

> ... of all possible crimes which an entire culture can commit, the one most difficult to bear, psychologically, is deicide. We live in a culture whose way of life testifies to the thoroughness with which the deity has been dispatched, but philosophers, writers, men of conscience everywhere squirm underneath the burden. For it is a far simpler matter to plot and commit a crime than it is to live with it afterwards.[23]

68 Living in the presence of the future

I leave the last word with philosopher Zygmunt Bauman:

> With the *pluralism* of rules (and our times are the times of pluralism) the moral choices (and the moral conscience left in their wake) appear to us intrinsically and irreparably *ambivalent*. Ours are the times of *strongly felt moral ambiguity*. These times offer us freedom of choice never before enjoyed, but also cast us into a state of uncertainty never before so agonising. We yearn for guidance we can trust and rely upon, so that some of the haunting responsibility for our choices could be lifted from our shoulders. But the authorities we may entrust are all contested, and none seems to be powerful enough to give us the degree of reassurance we seek. In the end we trust no authority, at least we trust none fully, and none for long: we cannot help being suspicious about any claim to infallibility. This is the most acute and practical aspect of what is justly described as the 'postmodern moral crisis'.[24]

4
Living with ourselves

A British television advertisement for a bank used to show people saying who they wanted to be. A traffic warden wanted to be loved. A New Ager wanted to be a tree. A small boy wanted to be a slug. A husband wanted to be a father, while his wife wanted to be alone. The message was simple: whoever we want to be, someone will lend us the money to make our dreams come true.

Who am I?

The search for ourselves is the cutting edge of postmodernity. To those in a position to receive its benefits it provides opportunities to play with our most treasured possession – our identity. It is ours to parade before the world, but it is also open to be formed, influenced and changed by social and cultural forces. This is the world in which Madonna changes her identity periodically and fashions change every season.

The essence of being or the question of what is a self has vexed philosophers and writers since ancient times. Perhaps there is a constant that makes me 'me', and spans a lifetime, and possibly beyond – a soul, as Christian philosophers would call it. Perhaps there is no constant, and I will be a completely different me when I am eighty. Perhaps I am totally the product of my past, my biology or my situation in life. Or perhaps I am no one person, but simply play whatever role fits in with my setting.

The questions we ask ourselves change as we age. When we are young we ask, 'What am I going to do with my life?' In mid-life it is, 'What am I doing with my life?' In old age we ask, 'What have I done with my life?' These questions assume that there are criteria by which we can judge our success or failure. Our answers may well plunge us into a period of anxious uncertainty, such as the 'mid-life crisis' that plagues many men. If there are criteria for judging our lives, the implications of our self-judgment can be heavy to bear. I may see myself, for instance, as being gifted musically, but feel that I have wasted that gift and in doing so ignored something that is an essential part of who I am. I have not been a good 'steward' of my gifts. I may have followed the wrong career, or alternatively, I may have accomplished more than I ever hoped for. Behind such reflections lies the issue of *vocation*. Is there one discernible path that I am meant to be following? If there is, is it possible to miss the path altogether?

This question could be seen as a luxury for those who have some degree of material well-being and control over their lives. How many millions of people spend each day trying to make a living in conditions of utter poverty or enslaved to the will of others? Nevertheless, these questions of identity and vocation have fascinated cultures of all kinds through the ages. Some traditional cultures regard the clan, tribe or extended family as the source of identity. Others, such as ours, have focused on the individual. In western society, the search for individual identity has been as much about allaying anxiety as about finding security. Identity is big business. We do psychological tests, such as Myers-Briggs, to discover our personality types, fill out questionnaires in popular magazines to determine what kind of member of the opposite sex would make a suitable partner for us, consult horoscopes, emulate the popular celebrities of our day, and choose fashions through which to express ourselves. Our questions about identity, failure and uncertainty fuel a burgeoning therapeutic culture. Yet when we are offered answers we ask, 'How can I possibly know that this is right?'

The Romantic self

Views of the self in our society have been drawn from many different sources. One is the Romanticism that flourished in the eighteenth and nineteenth centuries. Here people have 'soul'; they have emotional 'hidden depths', as well as an innate morality. Here too there is creativity, purpose and the possibility of deeply committed, even passionate, relationships. But the modern worldview threatens that outlook. Its emphasis on reason, objectivity and observation redirects our view of ourselves from passion to opinion, from relationship to systems and from spiritual metaphors to mechanistic models. It is this view that dominates our approach to science, government, the economy and education. Moreover, both the Romantic and the modern worldviews are being undermined by the postmodern. The very idea that people possess an identifiable fixed self is going.

The Romantic view of the self drew on Christian imagery to focus on the soul, which, even if it was not seen as sacred, at least referred to the 'deep interior'.[1] It was something deep inside every person which, though hidden from view, was a powerful force in human life and expression. Those for whom the soul expressed the divine image in humankind saw it as sacred, while others saw it as emotional power that could be either creative or destructive in its effects. For some, the soul and the emotions were one and the same thing. Love could be not only the highest expression of human relationship but also destructive of those very relationships. Friendship could be passionate and sacred, not only a meeting of minds but a twinning of souls.

In the modern world, passion became secularized and privatized. In previous ages the word 'passion' was most evident in its religious context, as in 'the passion of our Lord'. It came to describe the ecstasy of those who experienced God in ways that took them beyond their day-to-day existence.[2] The Romantics could still see passion as a 'sacred' force, even if it was stripped of its religious context. In the modern world it was to become almost entirely associated with sexuality, and was therefore inappropriate to describe friendship. Friendship could still be a lifetime commitment, but not a passionate one – at least in western culture. ('We're *just* friends.')

The modern self

The supremacy of reason over nature, which is one of the key themes of the modern world, had implications not only for the way we relate to the 'outer' world of society, but also for the way we relate to our 'inner' world – the world of the soul. Although much of our language is deeply influenced by the Romantic view of the self as embracing love, commitment, sacrifice, passion and the inner life, we have been influenced far more by the language and vision of the modern self. The adoption of the language of modernity was to affect every area of life. In the area of spirituality, for instance, it challenged the use of the imagination in meditating on the text of Scripture as part of the devotional life. Western Christianity was to become so imbued with rationalism that analysis of the biblical text would threaten meditation on it. Yet both are needed if the spiritual life is to be nurtured.

The idea that reason is the path to truth is a powerful one. On its foundations are built the institutions and professions of the modern world. Its claim to be the source of clarity, consistency and control has made it the dominant criterion of judgment in our society. Lesslie Newbigin suggested in his book *Foolishness to the Greeks* that the problem with the Enlightenment was that it eliminated the notion of purpose.[3] All effects can be explained by their causes, and this makes reason the essential tool for explanation. The modern self was sufficient by itself. It did not need God or his purposes to explain its own existence or its behaviour. When Friedrich Nietzsche announced that 'God is dead', he saw it as a statement about human freedom. God had to be obeyed. He punished and judged people, keeping them in servitude by requiring them to do his will. If there is no God, these things are no more. People are free to be themselves and to make their own decisions. Without God, humanity can grow up and explore the world for itself.

This implies two things. First, people have the potential to exercise their reason in the search for reality. And if they are to have the freedom to do so, they must also have the right to do so. Sociologist Charles Taylor has suggested that the western view of the self rests upon the principle of rights.[4] Thus, following the right to knowledge came the right to property, or the physical conditions in which to exercise the right to reason. The right to life also followed. The most famous statement of the rights of man, the American Declaration of Independence, affirmed the right to life, liberty and the pursuit of happiness. Taylor suggests that our present culture stands out in its treatment of the good life, or happiness, and that our moral thinking is built around three sub-principles: respect for others, a notion of the good life and an attitude of dignity.

The second point intertwines with the first. Modern man (the gender implications are intended) had not only rights but also had freedom. This was seen not only as freedom from duties towards God and his purposes, but as freedom to exercise his rights *and* as freedom from those aspects of his nature that threatened the dominance of reason. Philosopher Immanuel Kant is one of the primary proponents of this view. As sociologist Victor Seidler notes:

> For Kant freedom is essentially an issue of reason. We are free to the extent that we refuse to be influenced by our natures but use our reason to rise above them. Both our desires and our feelings, as well as the social relationships we live, are regarded by Kant as external, as parts of a nature that we have to learn to distance ourselves from. In contrast reason is taken to be an inner quality that is the source of our freedom and autonomy as individuals.[5]

Yet it can be said that modernity carried within itself the seeds of its own destruction, or of its own salvation, depending on how one views the outcome. The result of modernity was an all-powerful, rational self. It was resourceful and self-sufficient enough to have freedom and rights. In other words, it was an autonomous self that acted in the light of its own reason, without irrational impulses from within or from the external world.

Personal freedom also leads to one of the historical commitments of modernity – to social emancipation. A commitment to rights freed people from social contexts that were oppressive, representing as they did the unreasonable demands of institutions that denied them the right to live free lives. In the twentieth century the most obvious example of this was the emancipation of women, a direct application of the concepts of human rights and human freedoms. This oppression was attributed in part to the activities of the church in subjugating women as an expression of the divine will, and to the existence of patriarchy, which claimed that men alone were rational and women 'only' intuitive. Men had a superior claim to power since they could rise above such emotional states.

In separating itself from divine purpose, humanity also cut itself off from divine responsibility. In stating that everything could be explained by its causes, humanity gained responsibility for the ends of things as well. As theologian Colin Gunton says, 'It thus falls to the human agent not only to impose patterns of rationality on to recalcitrant nature, but to determine its future also.'[6] It was up to humanity to fill in the gap left by divine providence and purpose, replacing them with the idea of human progress. Of course, one of the effects of this was to give humanity a preoccupation with the future. This was to take the form not only of a commitment to material progress but also of a belief in moral progress. Both of these would eventually turn on modernity and wound it fatally.

But if reason is a function of the human mind over nature, what of the body? Descartes declared, 'I think, therefore I am.' How did he view the relationship between the mind and the body? Seidler comments:

> For Descartes the body is a part of the world of nature which is separated from reason and the mind which alone define our identities. The body is a machine that has to be used for it stands in an external relationship to our selves. The mind can no longer find a home in the world but has been estranged for as selves we have no place in the world. We can only find roots in our memories and so it is that within a modern philosophical tradition we learn to think of personal identity in terms of consciousness and mind.[7]

This picture of who we are is optimistic about self-control and reason, but distances our selves from nature, the body and loving human relationships. This view of humanity as above all rational suits that part of us that works towards objectives, that challenges problems, and that is committed to progress. It is not a view that fosters a holistic vision, or that integrates love and nature with rational decision-making. While evolutionists have challenged this separation of mind from nature, they have done so by seeing human beings as part of nature, which they have understood in mechanistic terms.

Colin Gunton identifies the tension between these two views of humanity – as distanced from nature and as part of it:

> ... it is one of the contradictions of modernity that side by side have developed a view of the person as essentially indistinguishable from, identical in being with, the non-personal universe, and a view of the person as so discontinuous with the matter of the world as to be an alien within it.[8]

Alienated the modern self may be, but at least it is not passive. The modern world may be like a game of Monopoly, characterized by competition and accumulation, but the pre-modern world was like a game of chess, with little or no change, in which identity was determined by tradition and power was always held by a hierarchy. Modernity's sense of being in control of one's own destiny meant that activity replaced contemplation. The fruits of this activity were soon to be found everywhere in society, and institutions were founded which reflected that activity and ensured that its impact was felt. In the modern world, therefore, the self may be alone as regards divine purpose, but it is not alone in terms of social change. It is constantly interacting with society and being shaped by it. Just as our actions have a global impact, changing the world, so those very changes affect the way we see ourselves and live our lives. Here is the essence of the local–global tension we have already discussed. We live in a *reflexive* world, in which the growth of knowledge, therapy, communications technology and the behaviour of our institutions cause us to alter our self-identity, which in turn shapes the society in which we live.

Vagabonds and tourists

Contrast the rational, controlling decision-maker of the modern world with, for instance, Zygmunt Bauman's pictures of contemporary men and women in a postmodern world. He chooses two pictures. One is the *vagabond*, the other the *tourist*.[9] The vagabond moves from place to place, not sure where he is going next, always moving on, never stopping for long:

What keeps him on the move is disillusionment with the place of the last sojourn and the forever smoldering hope that the next place that he has not visited yet, perhaps the place after the next, may be free from faults which repulsed him in the places he has already tasted. Pulled forward by hope untested, pushed from behind by hope frustrated ... the vagabond is a pilgrim without a destination; a nomad without an itinerary.[10]

Or, if you prefer, you could choose the picture of the tourist. The tourist is also a person with momentum, moving on all the time, interested not in the history of locations visited but only in their place in the tourist's own biography:

The tourists pay for their freedom; the right to disregard native concerns and feeling, the right to spin their own web of meanings, they obtain in a commercial transaction. Freedom comes in a contractual deal, the volume of freedom depends solely upon the ability to pay, and once purchased, it has become a right which the tourist can loudly demand, pursue through the course of the land and hope to be gratified and protected ... physically close spiritually remote: this is the formula of both the vagabond's and tourist's life.[11]

There is no sombre burdensome moral responsibility in either manner of life. Both are packaged and whisked away. With no responsibility for the evils of the places they visit, tourists are bad news for morality. They 'pass through'.

The multiphrenic self

But the postmodern self is not just about aimlessness. The crises of identity and vocation we are going through amount to more than this. American sociologist Kenneth Gergen has chronicled some of the pressures we face from the combination of modern and postmodern life in his book *The Saturated Self*. The technologies of communication have opened up to us so many new relationships and possibilities that we are losing our sense of our own identity, he says. We are saturated with an enormous amount of information about people and their lives from the media. Our circle of friends and acquaintances is growing all the time and is maintained by ever more efficient means of staying in contact with them. As well as this, we are offered the chance to play an ever-increasing number of roles. Our selves are 'populated' with many voices, so that we can choose who we are, who we could be or how we respond in any given context.

Each of these possibilities is given content as we gain information about them by watching them played out on our television screens night after night. The danger is that we imitate one another's attempts to play out the characters expected of us. Each of us is a repository of vast numbers of hidden potentials which come out when they are needed. Indeed, more and more is expected of us if we are to be seen to be living a fulfilled life. Ambitious, entertaining, good at cooking, warm friend, able to fix the car, someone who appreciates music, sport or art, a good lover – each of these roles may figure in our lives, and we may feel under pressure to give an impression that we are all of these persons if the circles we mix in require it. These are our 'possible selves', and we may change according to the context in which we find ourselves. The adventure of exploring the technologies of communication gives us seemingly endless possibilities to be different people, whether in the internet chat room, communicating by email across the world, or receiving information on which we can act or to which we can react. The whole process becomes an ever-widening circle over which we spread our selves. 'Mutiphrenia', 'many-mindedness', is the condition of making numerous 'self-investments' in all directions.

Kenneth Gergen highlights three issues that arise from this. First, we need to develop 'coping skills'. The more we 'want', the less we are free from 'not wanting'. We desire more, but we can become enslaved to desire itself. Our goals expand, our interests accumulate and our lives fill up. We watch football, read French novels, and enjoy gastronomy, gardening and DIY. We get frustrated because there is not enough time to follow these interests as much as we would like and work also is stressful. We have to 'find time' for these activities and put effort into them. As far as we can, we also keep up with friends, to whom we owe debts of hospitality and care. If we go on holiday together – an opportunity to 'relax' – we have to make a hundred and one preparations before we can get away. Gergen says that 'liberation becomes a swirling vertigo of demands'.[12]

Secondly, Gergen points out that we all have a sense of 'ought', which comes from our upbringing. Parents, teachers, clergy and others all teach us how to live the 'good life'. But the tasks we are called to do by our society, and in which we are meant to invest ourselves, can be at odds with what we feel we ought to be doing. We may feel inadequate, for instance, because we pursue hobbies when we could be doing much worthier things with our lives. We are beset by the tension between what we do and what we feel we should be doing:

> Each voice of value stands to discredit all that does not meet its standard. All the voices at odds with one's current conduct thus stand as internal critics, scolding, ridiculing and robbing action of its potential for fulfillment.[13]

Thirdly, Gergen argues that what is rational or reasonable depends on the group context. In one group smoking is exciting, but in another it is dangerous. In one culture we marry for love; in another by arrangement. Each has its own rationale. Each relationship we form adds to the number of possible ways of living, so the idea of an obvious solution to a problem disappears. There are as many acceptable answers to a problem as there are groups within which it is discussed. Eventually, a rationally coherent position becomes impossible and therefore arbitrary. The degree of complexity we find ourselves in makes rational choice meaningless. Gergen concludes:

> So we find a profound sea-change taking place in the character of social life during the twentieth century. Through an array of newly emerging technologies the world of relationships becomes increasingly saturated. We engage in greater numbers of relationships, in a greater variety of forms, and with greater intensities than ever before. With the multiplication of relationships also comes a transformation in the social capacities of the individual – both in knowing how

and knowing that. The relatively coherent and unified sense of self inherent in a traditional culture gives way to manifold and competing potentials. A multiphrenic condition emerges in which one swims in ever-shifting, concatenating and contentious currents of being. One bears the burden of an increasing array of oughts, of self-doubts and irrationalities. The possibility for committed romanticism or strong and single-minded modernism recedes, and the way is opened up for the postmodern being.[14]

This view of the self is possible in a world where objective truth has given way to a multiplicity of voices. The idea that we can know ourselves because God knows us and made us is a million miles away from this cacophony of voices and the confusion they bring. Gergen accurately portrays something of the confusion of the postmodern self. This is a world where there can be no certainty of vocation, and where people frequently change what they are doing with their lives in search of some aspect of fulfilment that is eluding them. Listening to the voices becomes an exhausting and ultimately frustrating way of living. But those who celebrate postmodernity see it as a liberating way of life. Anything is possible. You can be who you want to be, when you want to be. Indeed, you can also become me as we interact with each other. Postmodernism is most vulnerable when asked how it judges between different worldviews. There is no God or objective value system to enable that to be done. In Gergen's opinion, modernists see postmodernism as rejecting reason as the basis of decision-making, while Romanticists see it as a rejection of an essentially moral commitment.

But postmodernists argue that the problems of the world are due not to relativism but to precisely those 'ethically' or 'rationally' superior standpoints that Romanticism and modernism engender. Such standpoints give rise to conflict and civil strife. Gergen argues that postmodernism is therefore good for the world:

> With the full flowering of postmodernism, the very concept of 'foundational conflicts' between good and evil, true and false, rational and irrational would dwindle into obscurity. To silence, incarcerate, or kill adherents of different political,

religious, economic or ethical discourses (and their related practices) would cease to make sense. Such actions would be akin to Wagner-lovers burning the works of Verdi, baseball fans setting terrorist bombs in football stadiums, or Chinese gourmands sending freedom fighters to liberate the guests at French restaurants.[15]

Here again, we encounter that unconditional tolerance which is such a key 'virtue' of postmodern culture. Social saturation has made us a part of one another to such an extent that we have become 'populated with the identities of others'. This makes us aware of our own 'relational embeddedness', and because we can see the perspective of others more clearly, war between people becomes a nonsense.

It may well be that the Enlightenment claimed too much when it asserted the possibility of certain knowledge. Postmodernity may be seen as a reaction to something that should never have been promised in the first placed. Christianity, as we shall see, does not equate faith with scientific certainty about God. To enjoy faith is to take a risk. But one of the outcomes of that faith (and therefore of that risk) is the ability to state that I know who I am, even though I am discovering more about myself every day. This enables me to resist false potential personas that do not appropriately express my self. It enables me to seek wisdom to guide me in my vocational life. It also provides for repentance and forgiveness when I make a mistake. In postmodernity there seems to be no basis for repentance, because there is no moral measure against which I may judge whether or not I have done wrong.

Spirituality with a small 's'?

In our culture there is an increasing interest in spirituality with a small 's'. A world based on reason alone cannot satisfy people who are made in the image of God. But much of the new spirituality is irrational as far as traditional religions are concerned. New Age mysticism protests against the modern world. Andrew Greeley puts it well:

> The tribal Gods are being worshipped once again in

substantial part as a protest against the hyperrationist society and the failures of that society. There are few better ways of rejecting science than turning to astrology; few more effective ways of snubbing the computer than relying on Tarot cards; and few better ways of coping with rationalist 'liberal' college professors than putting hexes on them.[16]

One development is an increased interest in paganism, especially among young people. Thousands of internet sites are dedicated to witchcraft, according to a recent article by Marina Baker, and New Age shops are feeding young people's desire to set up groups to perform the rites and rituals of the 'craft'. One adult witch who is currently publishing a handbook for 'young witches' claims that the average age for those interested is thirteen for girls and seventeen for boys. According to Baker,[17] paganism is big business in our society and challenges contemporary Christianity to think again about its failure to reach young people.

Baker suggests that young people get attracted to paganism through their increased awareness of green issues. Paganism brings together concern for the Earth with a sense of power. It is fuelled by positive media images and commercial exploitation, and offers a sense of mystery and excitement which organized religion does not. It is easy to see all this as harmless fun, and perhaps it is a passing fad for many, but the rise of paganism with its male and female gods, its spells and rituals, is filling a spiritual vacuum. It draws people away from an understanding of the God who made the Earth and replaces the creator with age-old idolatry.

The West often borrows spiritualities from different cultures or worldviews. For example, the ways of life of indigenous peoples such as American Indians and Aborigines are 'consumed' by westerners as time away from the pressures of ordinary life. They feature in retreats or holidays, or are used in times of crisis by people whose lives are wholly industrial or post-industrial. In fact, our approach to such spiritualities is largely related to their usefulness to us. Do they fit in with what we want? Do they fill a gap in our culture's experience of life? Perhaps it is accurate to see our attitude to such spiritualities as another form of leisure consumption. After all, our fascination with them comes and goes. They follow fashion trends, as do other consumer items. They do not hold the same meanings for us as they do for the indigenous peoples.

Some of the recent interest in spirituality in the Christian world is of the same nature. Think of the recent influence of Gregorian chant, the writings of Julian of Norwich and Celtic myths and traditions. Each of these is, in itself, an important part of Christian tradition. But within our own 'cut-and-paste' culture (the tourist's scrapbook), an eclectic spirituality is now at the leading edge of our mission to the world.

The term 'spirituality' is very hard to define. Spirituality, like love, has been made into a commodity. It exhibits a strange mixture of modernity and postmodernity. It is still modern in that it uses the language of technique and experts, yet it is postmodern in that it is a 'pick-your-own', individualistic mixture. It is not only the church as a whole that has to be aware of these attitudes. Individual Christians also have to guard against the cut-and-paste culture.

Evangelicals have always stressed the need for personal faith and the importance of living out that faith in the world. But both head and heart must be engaged as we live out our faith. One reason evangelicals have sometimes been suspicious of the idea of spirituality is because of its emphasis on the interior life. This emphasis, it has been felt, serves to strengthen the divide between the sacred and the secular, between those pursuits deemed spiritual (mostly connected with religion) and those of a lower order. But genuine spirituality aims at an integrated life in which everything we do is related to the existence of God. The lack of such spirituality implies that there is no need for relatedness to God, who is seen as separate from the world. To be spiritual is to live with integrity in the world, in relationship with God. Spirituality is not a 'special' thing, but is about the ordinary and the everyday. It is not about intense or profound experiences, but is about our lifelong quest to know God and at the same time to know ourselves, since it is impossible to disentangle our knowledge of God from our knowledge of ourselves. Spirituality is about friendship as much as about prayer. Indeed, to learn about friendship will lead us to learn more about prayer. The more we realize this, the more we shall see prayer, not as an onerous activity to be got through, but as a response to God which comes out of living in his presence.

Separating our knowledge of God from our knowledge of ourselves leads to problems. If we emphasize only our relationship with God, we may find it difficult to root our Christian faith in our ordinary lives. After all, we are people who struggle, get frustrated and often misunderstand what is happening to us. If we see God only as transcendent, our faith will not be rooted. We may stress the divine so much that we are left feeling inadequate because our own lives never measure up to what is expected of us. We are meant to have daily times of devotion, but our stressed lives may not make space for them, so we feel guilty. We may make the mistake of going elsewhere for help with difficulties that arise out of our human frailties, regarding Christianity as unable (or unwilling) to help us with them. Yet if we focus only on ourselves and on our human development as the measure of our faith, we neglect our partnership with God and lose the liberty that comes through an understanding of grace. Knowing God and knowing ourselves belong together. Pursuing the knowledge of God without self-knowledge leads to the incomprehensible, while the reverse leads us into therapy.

In *The Color Purple*, Alice Walker's main character Celie is on a journey of self-discovery, in which she has a conversation with her lover Shuh about God. Shuh suggests:

God love everything you love – and a mess of stuff you don't. But more than anything else, God love admiration. You saying God vain? I ast. Naw, she say. Not vain, just wanting you share a good thing. I think it pisses God off if you walk by the color purple in a field somewhere and don't notice it. What it do when it pissed off? I ast. Oh, it make something else. People think pleasing God is all God care about. But any fool living in the world can see it always trying to please us back. Yeah? I say. Yeah, she say. It always making little surprises and springing them on us when we least expect.[18]

Spirituality does of course include understanding the tradition we received on our conversion. If we remain ignorant of what it means to be a Christian, we may suffer unnecessarily, or reinvent the wheel rather than learning from the wisdom of the past. But spirituality is also about an ongoing relationship with God marked by togetherness, affection, respect, faithfulness and affirmation. God has given us the gift of reason through which we can unlock the tradition, and the gift of imagination through which we can experience the relationship. We have not been cut adrift. We have been drawn into a relationship which is the very basis of our identity and vocation – and of man–woman relationships, as we shall see in the next chapter.

5
Living in relationship

Central to a Christian perspective on the relationship between men and women is our interdependence. Our complementarity and our essential need for relationship and community lie at the heart of our humanity. The fundamental statement of this is contained in the creation narratives in Genesis 1 and 2. Here we find that the person made out of the dust was lonely. God said of that person, 'It is not good for the man to be alone.' Though many animals populated the planet, there was no companionship. The story that God took the rib from Adam's side and made a woman is remarkable in what it reveals about us. It shows that we share a common and equal humanity. It also shows that individualism is an inadequate way of life for human beings. We need relationship, and relationship depends on diversity. Woman is different from man. Adam's cry 'bone of my bones and flesh of my flesh' is the basis of both recognition and respect: recognition of what we have in common, and respect for what is different. If the person created out of Adam had been the same as him, his isolation would be replicated. If they were completely different, there would have been no resonance. The relationship is reciprocal and mutual. Each freely and independently gives to the other. Each needs the other and is not complete without the other. They belong to each other and conduct a continuous exploratory conversation with each other through life. There is no place for monologue (talking at), but only dialogue (talking with).

Another reason for the existence of both man and woman is the trinitarian nature of God. God is three persons in one: Father, Son and Holy Spirit. They live together in perfect community. The doctrine of the Trinity requires us to balance the indivisibility of God with the distinctiveness of the three persons of the Godhead. Each of the three persons has a common nature but holds that nature uniquely. God is love in action. The Father loves the Son, who loves the Holy Spirit. In a one-person world there would be no love because there would be no-one to love. 'It is not good for the man to be alone', not only for the sake of the man's isolation, but also because relationship is part and parcel of being made in the image of God.

> God created us 'male *and* female'; that is, in sexual encounter rather than in simple opposition. Both creation accounts affirm that it is only through this encounter, through the *and* which unites the different, that life may be called human, an image of God.[1]

This relationship with God is essential to understanding what it means to be human. It comes before the discussion of our social relationships. It is because we understand something of the relationships within God that we can assert that our identity is essentially relational rather than individual. We are defined by our relationship to the 'other'. Whatever it means to be a self, it is about being in relationship. As theologian Anthony Thiselton writes about the influence of Schelling, 'he paved the way for the notion that encountering the strange, the alien, the unfamiliar, the different, in short the Other, is a pre-condition for interpreting and understanding persons and selfhood'.[2]

Once we know that our identity is formed by our relationship to God and to others, we can ask what kind of relationships should exist among ourselves. The relationship between the man and the woman in the creation stories established the pattern for all relationships between human beings, not just for those between men and women. The idea of interdependence, mutual respect and common recognition, and the fact that we need one another and need to give to one another, lie at the heart of all human community. These things are not expressed in male–female relationships alone.

With this in mind, it is worth looking at friendship in general before examining relationships between men and women further. Theologian Jürgen Moltmann speaks in very down-to-earth terms of 'open friendship', which, in its widest sense, is a relationship with anything waiting to be discovered:

> Friendship is a way of behaving that makes no claims. 'Friend' is not an official title, or a role we have to play, or a function in society ... friendships grow up out of free encounter. Friendship is a personal relationship between people who like one another. Friendship combines *affection with respect*.[3]

Friendship is the ultimate safe space in which to stop playing our roles and to take off our masks. It is about being liked for existing, not for being useful. Friendship, Moltmann also points out, is about faithfulness along the way. It is about throwing open free spaces for our friend by unconditionally affirming him or her.

The relationship between the man and the woman is one instance of that kind of friendship. But of course the relationship between the man and the woman is informed by their sexuality and by their expression of it in sexual intercourse. Yet sexuality only represents their whole relationship with one another. It is a part of their mutuality and of their ongoing encounter with each other. Where the act of sex is mere genital activity and does not require this greater commitment, it is impossible to talk of sexual fulfilment. Rather, there is sexual alienation, since the manner in which the act is performed denies the possibility of any exploration of being male *and* female together.

This open conversation between humanity and God and between male and female is conducted, not in the confines of abstract theology, but in the concrete context of the everyday and the ordinary. In other words, it is lived out through the body. The Bible does not list those sex and gender characteristics that have dominated the interaction between men and women for so long. But it does provide us with a vision of how things should be, and of how they were before they went wrong.

This high calling, given in Eden, was fragile. The relationship between men and women was broken by the introduction of evil into the world. In Genesis 3 we find the relationship of men and women, as well as their roles, fundamentally changed. Before the fall, men and women were equal. But now power replaces equality as the man rules the wife, who submits to that power. Instead of both working alongside one another, working out the mandate to be stewards of the earth's resources, they are separated into different roles. The man is sent to work in the public domain, where nature now gives up its riches grudgingly. The woman is sent into the private domain, where childbirth and the raising of children have become painful and frustrating rather than unequivocally joyful. The fact that these things happened after the fall shows that they were not part of God's original intentions. They belong to the disaster that has befallen the world. The rest of the Bible tells the story of how God sets out to renew the world, to redeem its people, and to restore the relationship between men and women.

That relationship now contains the explosive ingredients of power, submission and frustration. Restoring the relationship needs to be worked at as much as the tilling of the ground or the raising of children. There is a constant need to forgive one another and to preserve that recognition and respect without which the relationship will blow apart. The Mosaic law protected women and restrained men from abusing their power, but it was only the coming of Christ and his explanation of what it means to live in the kingdom of God that brought fundamental change.

Ignoring the Trinity and the kingdom of God has had a devastating impact on our society. Moltmann writes:

> The disappearance of the social doctrine of the Trinity has made room for the development of individualism, and especially 'possessive individualism', in the western world: everyone is supposed to fulfill 'himself' but who fulfills the community? It is a typically western bias to suppose that social relationships and society are less 'primal' than the person.[4]

God addresses us in the context of the society we live in. We cannot avoid being in relationship with God, since we are made in the divine image. But we can reject the call of God and, instead of working to redeem human relationships, exacerbate the divide between us. In what follows I offer a brief narrative of the recent revolution in the way men and women relate to one another and consider why it is that men and women have become so alienated from one another.

Changing gender

The twentieth century saw enormous and fundamental changes in the relationships between men and women, in the roles they play in the family and the community, and in the way we perceive ourselves as well as one another. Perhaps it was inevitable that in a rapidly changing world nothing would be exempt from change. Over the century, the two world wars, votes for women, their entry into the labour market, changes in technology, and contraception all changed the relationships between men and women. Looking back from after the end of the century to the beginning, it is difficult to imagine that all those changes took place in the space of a hundred years. Although the extension of the franchise to women was perhaps the most significant moment in those changes, the most turbulent time came after the end of the Second World War.

With men at war, women were drafted in to do the work they had left behind. To encourage women to go to work, the government opened up a thousand nurseries. Women worked in factories making bombers, in the civil service and in all walks of life where there was any need for workers. While the men were fighting, the women were working, and as they did so they discovered new abilities of which they had been unaware. When the men came back from the war, life resumed. The nurseries were closed, sending a potent message to women to return to their domestic duties. But life did not return to normal. Something had changed both in the men and in the women. Yet the 1950s started out as a conservative decade. It was a time when 'men were men and women were women', with extreme stereotypes of both. Women were characterized by their exceptional femininity and their willingness to submit to their men. Men were 'in charge' both at work and as 'head of the household' in the home. It was said that men served industry and women served men.

It was as if something was being suppressed. If it was, the most likely candidate was women's new awareness that they were capable of doing more than running a home or looking after children. There seemed no way of realizing any such ambitions, however, while women's identity was so bound up in bearing children. The means of limiting families were unreliable, and running a home without the technology of convenience gave women very little time for anything else. The conservative nature of society meant that any women breaking ranks risked being ostracized.

During this period the roles, characteristics and occupations of men and women could be represented in two parallel columns, one headed 'Men' and the other 'Women'. Under the column headed 'Men' were roles such as head of household, disciplinarian, decision-maker and planner. Here also were listed the trades and professions that showed men excelling in public life, the manipulation of ideas and of materials, the use of strength and the cause of honour. They were lawyers, politicians, miners, doctors, policemen, architects, clergy, carpenters or steelworkers. These occupations were men's work, not women's. Underwriting these roles and occupations were the characteristics of the male gender as rational, controlling, strong, direct and protective. Men dealt with their emotions privately; they were brave and sacrificial, and showed love by what they did for those they loved.

Women had another list. Here were the roles of wife and mother, supporter and carer, the occupations of homemaker, child-bearer, and, by extension, of nurse and teacher. Women were intuitive, vulnerable carers. Submissiveness to men meant that working roles for single women were approved as long as they worked under men in positions such as waitresses or secretaries, and did not usurp positions held by men. It was this kind of society that Simone de Beauvoir saw as being oppressive in her influential work *The Second Sex*.[5] The culture behaved as if men and women were in different compartments. It was difficult for both men and women to cross the divide between the two worlds represented by the two lists.

But by the end of the 1950s things had begun to change. With the advent of rock and roll and the culture that grew up around it, the idea of 'counter-culture' took hold. The idea that conservative 'family' values were in some sense a given (although no culture is monolithic) began to be challenged. The possibility of bringing about change by challenging authority itself was to become a persistent theme in the years to come. The beginnings of rebellion by the new so-called 'teenagers' cracked the acceptability of patriarchy. Men could no longer 'control' children, who no longer wanted to be the same as their parents. Women began to see that the culture of the two lists, though it might have brought stability and certainty to the home and the community, did so at the expense of personal freedom. In an age of human rights, what choices did women have compared to men? What seemed to have been the natural order of things began to be seen as suppression and, as the personal became political, as oppression.

It is important to call what happened in the 1960s a revolution. During that period the protest by young people against all that their parents' generation stood for affected every area of life. Not only did teenagers challenge the authority of their parents, and specifically of their fathers (since the father was traditionally the authority figure in the household), but they also challenged patriarchy itself. This attempt to expose a free society as a 'front' for patriarchal imperialism needed a new political language, and this was found in socialism and the words of Marx, Lenin and Mao. There was much to criticize. One of the most telling acts during this period was the way in which the American protest movement focused attention on the failings of the political establishment by its campaigns against the Vietnam War and also against racial injustice in the United States. The rebellion of many may have been mild, and some never broke away from the values of their parents' generation, but western culture was never the same again.

This period also saw the women's liberation movement become a major force, not only among women but also as a political movement in its own right. In 1970 the first national Women's Liberation conference was held at Ruskin College, Oxford, and Germaine Greer's book *The Female Eunuch* was published. Its emphasis was on the liberation of women from male oppression. It was not just liberation *from*, however, but liberation *for*. Gradually, employment opportunities opened up for women. Laws, such as the British Sex Discrimination Act 1975 made it illegal for employers to discriminate against women. Even golf clubs had to admit women, though many did so grudgingly. Although the pace of change was in some respects slow, it became obvious that women were men's equals in many areas of work previously considered a male preserve by virtue of biology. It began to be clear that not all the differences between men and women were biological; some were due to the social construction of gender. We had become saturated with myths, expectations and narratives by which we made sense of sex and gender. Indeed, sex and gender began to be treated as being in tension with each other, the one favouring biology, the other the social construction of reality. Maleness and masculinity separated out, as did femaleness and femininity. 'Femininity' began to carry negative connotations for feminists, as it was seen as the projection of masculine fantasies about women on to women.

During this period, women's liberation also adopted the language of socialism as the only available alternative to a traditional and conservative worldview. Gradually, the theme of liberation changed into that of equality, with its economic and socio-cultural connotations. No-one seemed to notice the replacement of the one by the other. But the concept of equality carried with it a hidden agenda – the notion that women should conform to male patterns of behaviour. The idea that men and women were essentially different may well have been a hallmark of patriarchy, but the idea that men and women were essentially the same was also problematic. The revolution of the 1960s was reactive, and the pendulum was still swinging. The measured statement that men and women were *both* same *and* different was not strong enough to express the need for change.

Equality of opportunity threatened to become equality of identity. The two lists merged to become one. Ironically, it was during this period that the concept of gender identity was most under threat, becoming subsumed in an androgynous concept of the person. The roles, characteristics and occupations previously separated into two were now one list, and anybody could borrow from them. But whereas before there had been certainty without freedom, now there was freedom without certainty. Postmodernity added to this uncertainty, as the givens that had been the reference points for self-identity began to disappear and the idea of constructing one's own identity began to take hold. The idea that there were areas in which women's capabilities may be inferior to those of men became 'no go' areas. This became a recurrent issue during the 1970s and 1980s as 'politically correct' tolerance became a threat to free speech by establishing a new kind of intolerance of those who held the old conservative agenda.

The challenge to masculinity

These changes had an impact on the way men viewed themselves and their relationships with women. In a patriarchal world, men could ignore gender issues and even be unaware of their own gender. My own recent research on this topic reached the remarkable conclusion that many men thought of themselves as a person but not as men, and had never thought about their own masculinity.[6] Women, as the deviation from the patriarchal norm, were most aware of their gender. Although a majority in demographic terms, they were a minority in cultural terms. But then the women's movement held up a mirror to men's view of themselves and said, 'This is who you really are. This is how we see you.' This brought masculinity sharply into view and compelled men to deal with it. This process, which began in the 1970s and then gathered pace in the 1980s, was sometimes described as the 'men's movement', but in reality it was no such thing. Women had demonstrated that they could change society through their collective empathy and their sense of solidarity with one another. They were 'sisters under the skin'. They faced the challenge of *oppression*. But men found that they were isolated from one another and that one of the main challenges they faced was their difficulty of *expression*. It was true that men bonded easily in terms of doing sport or other activities together, but they remained isolated from one another at an emotional level. They became stereotyped as the gender out of touch with its emotions.

This was important, because being in touch with your emotions had become the currency of society. Men who, in a previous generation, had loved by sacrificing their lives or by working in demeaning jobs to feed their families were asked to share their feelings. The currency of this culture was intimacy, but that seemed unattainable, judging by the rate at which relationships were breaking up.

Men started to face a crisis of identity. This reflected their response to the two issues at the heart of the progress of women, namely employment and fertility. Men had traditionally seen themselves as protectors, providers and procreators. In peacetime, the latter two were the most important reference points for male identity. Men were those who provided for the family. The world of work was the main source of male identity, but it was a fragile world susceptible to change with the business cycle, redundancy being seen as the consequence of failure. As women joined the labour market, the percentage of men in employment did not change. With advances in technology, machines replaced men with basic skills. The economy began to favour service industries, and since work was moving from being hierarchically organized to network-based, relational skills became more important. The majority of new jobs became part-time[7] and were aimed at women.

Despite the problems women were facing in terms of discrimination at work, men began to see that whereas women had added something to their lives, men themselves had lost something. Women now had more options than before, having added the world of work to the domain of the home. Books started to appear with such titles as *Can Women Have it All?*, yet at the same time women discussed the stress they felt at having to juggle work and home life.

Some communities emptied during the day as the majority of people went out to work. Neighbourliness became less prevalent. Paid, but not usually residential, helpers who, in a previous age, would have been called servants, were reintroduced into the home as nannies, housekeepers, gardeners and cleaners, to do what its owners had no time to do. The *General Household Survey* of 1999 showed that half of all British parents who made term-time arrangements for pre-school children, and most of those making such arrangements for school-age children, relied on family or friends at least part of the time. Some people had to get their children up early to travel long distances to the nursery or school of their choice before going to work, picking them up late in the afternoon or early evening, perhaps from an after-school club. The myth of the latch-key child became prevalent, although it does seem to have been more of a myth than a reality: only 7% of parents with children aged 6–18 reported that their children came home to an empty house, compared with 9% who said that *they* did so as children.[8] Of families with children, 44% ate together every day, while 9% never did so.[9]

Such statistics became a source of fascination as people compared their own lifestyle with that of others. Time had undoubtedly become the new scarce resource. The unemployed spent time to save money, and the jugglers spent money to save time. The redundant were depressed and the jugglers were stressed. It soon became clear that you could not have it all, but no-one seemed willing to let the cat out of the bag.

One problem was that some men were not doing their share of the management of the home.[10] Many women were having to work, care for the children and manage the home. Some feminists accused men of conspiring to make women so stressed that they would capitulate *en masse* and head back for homemaking and childcare, as in the 'good old days'. Though this may have been the agenda of a few men, there was no sign that it represented the views of most. Those in work were increasingly under pressure to deliver as the demands of international competition swept aside job security. Both men and women were expected to work long hours to stay on top of their jobs. But women in particular worried about balancing the competing demands of home and work, especially when completing work meant working at home in the evenings.

A survey conducted by the University of Bristol for a BBC *Panorama* documentary in January 2000[11] showed that of 560 women returning to work after the birth of their first child, 36% had left their job within two years, 17% having switched to part-time work and 19% having given up work altogether. A smaller survey,[12] conducted by the University of Sussex, showed that women who did return to full-time employment did so when their children were very young and tended to work very long hours. Researcher Susan Harkness commented that 'there was no reduction in hours prior to and after the birth of the child'. There was 'no accommodation within their jobs to account for the fact that they now had responsibilities for a very young child'. Many women found it impossible to combine having a child with the demands of a working life, especially when their employment was based on rigid, male patterns of working. The adoption of 'family-friendly' working conditions seemed to be progressing slowly, and stress levels for working women with children were high. In 2000, the birth of a child to Cherie Blair, a senior barrister and the wife of Prime Minister Tony Blair, increased the emphasis on the need for 'family-friendly policies'.

In these circumstances women are having fewer children, a rational decision given their conditions of employment and the consequent domestic stress. They are also having them later in life. Some career women decide at a young age that they will not have children, knowing that motherhood would be incompatible with their career. In the words of one such woman, 'If you want to have a career, you must work the same hours as everybody else, which means pretending that you do not have a child.' One of the key issues at stake here is the flexibility of work for both men and women. If patterns of work change significantly, this will substantially reduce the stress levels experienced by both, but particularly by women. Meanwhile, the main change in patterns of work is the job insecurity induced by globalization, and the subsequent collapse of the concept of the career.

Whether they want to have children or not, women have childbearing as a biological reference point on which to base personal identity. Male identity tends to be socially constructed around the workplace. A woman can work and then leave to have children; a man cannot. In the days when men worked and women bore children, the stability that resulted was due not only to oppression but also to the fact that both sexes had secure gender identities. Of course, men can become house-husbands, looking after the children in the home, but research shows that this appeals only to a tiny minority of men. Being a father is an essential part of masculine identity, and many men do see fatherhood as the focus of their masculinity; but they still see bringing up children in the home, especially in their early years, as predominantly a woman's job, even if they regard themselves as equal partners in parenting. There is evidence that men who are married and in the home are spending more time with their children, not only being available to them (being in their vicinity), but also being actively engaged with them. Meanwhile, a women's conference held in 1997 summarized the factors that had most changed women's lives in the twentieth century as the Pill, the right to vote, and the washing machine.

The crisis in masculinity which came to the fore in the 1980s and 1990s seemed at first to be economic in origin. It was due to the loss of distinctive work-based identity, as well as to the trend for the labour market to favour women as the new employees. By the end of 2001 in the UK more women will be in work than men. This seems to be borne out by the changes in relative incomes for men and for women. Lionel Tiger, Professor of Anthropology at Rutgers University, says of the US:

> All told, there is a significant shift in the relative power of men and women. In the United States productive system in the mid-nineties women earned 7.6% more than they did in 1979, while men earned 14% less than they did then. Women earn 40% of family income. In the early 1990s at least one of six wives earned more than her husband; in 1968 it was one in eighteen. According to Gail Sheehy,[13] by 1996 nearly one of three wives earned more than her husband.[14]

But this is not enough to explain why all this started to happen in the 1960s, nor why it has happened so quickly rather than being a gradual process. To explain this, we need to investigate the situation in more detail. We can begin by looking at the recent thinking of political philosopher Francis Fukuyama.

The great disruption

Francis Fukuyama has become one of the leading political philosophers of our generation. He has written about some of the key issues of our day with a combination of academic rigour and clarity of thought that has made his books widely read. His ideas about the future of liberal democracy will be discussed in the next chapter. In his recent book, *The Great Disruption: Human Nature and the Reconstitution of Social Order*,[15] he analyses the way society changed rapidly over the last half of the twentieth century. He looks at changes in 'social capital', which he defines as 'the existence of a certain set of informal values or norms shared among members of a group that permit co-operation among them'.[16] Social capital depends on virtues such as truth-telling and the meeting of

98 Living in the presence of the future

obligations. In the West these have strong links with the Puritan movement and the Reformation.

One difficulty in making social capital the essential tool for social analysis is that it is not easy to measure. Fukuyama gets round this by assessing the *absence* of social capital, using traditional measures of social deviance. There are problems with this, and Fukuyama admits that using social deviance as a proxy for social capital is similar to using poverty data as a measure of a society's overall wealth. Nevertheless, he goes on to use this method to chronicle the breakdown of society.

His argument is sophisticated and he weaves several themes together. It is therefore impossible, and maybe unfair, to isolate one theme. But one theme is central to his main argument and has a bearing on our analysis in this chapter: the decline of the nuclear family. He uses statistics that demonstrate the escalation of both divorce and illegitimacy in Britain throughout the century,[17] comparing both to statistics from other OECD[18] countries over the last thirty years. He then presents statistics for crime (both homicide and property crime) and mentions child abuse as well as substance abuse. His thesis is that we have lived through 'a great disruption', which has had a devastating impact on civil society in the West.

In arriving at possible explanations for the marked increases in social deviancy that his figures suggest, he hangs a great deal on the role of the family. He frames his thesis within the controversial paradigm of evolutionary biology, the context for his discussion of the different psychologies of men and women. From this point of view, the aim of an organism is to pass on its genes to the next generation. This requires distinct strategies for men and for women:

> ... for females, reproductive strategy involves commanding sufficient economic resources to protect themselves and the offspring until the latter are able to take care of themselves. Males, by contrast, require a far lower level of parental investment to get their genes into the next generation and their strategy therefore involves spreading their genes as widely as possible.[19]

Women tend to emphasize the quality of their mates, whereas

men tend to emphasize quantity. It is an old cliché. Fukuyama sees the decline of the family as heavily influenced by a breakdown in the traditional exchange of fertility (controlled by the female) for economic resources (almost always controlled by the male). Fukuyama supports the conservative argument that this breakdown arises not from economic deprivation, or from problems of dependency induced by welfare programmes, but from the cultural shift that took place in the 1960s. This shift has been well documented. The main question is whether it was self-generating or whether it was itself caused by more basic socio-economic forces. Fukuyama views with suspicion the idea that this shift was autonomous, since, whereas most cultural changes take place slowly, the 1960s saw the start of a fundamental change in attitudes which completely altered the nature of family life over two or three decades.

Before the shift, a husband was required to turn over a substantial part of his earnings to his wife, reflecting the seriousness of his lifelong commitment to her and their children. If a man got a woman pregnant, he was expected to marry her, reinforcing the exchange of fertility for resources.

Two things happened to change this dependency of women (and their children) on men. First, advances in birth control and abortion procedures enabled women to control their own rate of childbirth. The main effect of birth control was not that it lowered fertility but that it removed the risks associated with sexual intercourse, and this changed male behaviour at the same time. The number of 'shot-gun marriages declined substantially'. Fukuyama says: '… since the pill permitted women to have sex without worrying about economic consequences, men felt liberated from norms requiring them to look after the women they had got pregnant'.[20]

Secondly, as we have seen, women increasingly participated in the labour force and saw their incomes rise relative to those of men. The rise in female incomes added to the cultural shift by enabling women to support themselves and their children without husbands. But this further weakened the norm of male responsibility. As men became increasingly unreliable, women acquired job skills so as to be even less dependent on them. Thus the whole cycle became self-reinforcing.

Fukuyama's argument is supported by US data, but Japan is an exception in that Japanese divorce rates have moved up only slightly, while illegitimacy, crime and social deviance indicators have actually moved down. Fukuyama sees Japan as different because female incomes in Japan are low compared to those of men. Japanese women are still dependent on men. Added to this is the fact that the Pill was legalized in Japan as late as 1996, so that Japanese women have had little control over their reproductive cycles.

Fukuyama states that he is not underplaying the impact of changes in religious or moral values. But, in his view, these are not enough to explain the sudden changes evident in statistics throughout the western world. If it is true, as evolutionary psychology suggests, that male attitudes to children are socially constructed whereas female attitudes to them are rooted in biology, this may explain current masculine behaviour. Women can afford to be less selective in their choice of partners, and men can abandon wife and children, with less negative consequences. This change and its consequences cannot be blamed on women. It is important to emphasize the increasing irresponsibility of men as they have walked away from their relationships.

In particular, the absence of fathers has had an incalculable effect on children. Both sons and daughters suffer from the absence of a male role-model in the home. Daughters suffer because of the lack of a relationship with a man upon which they can base relationships with men later in life. Sons suffer through the lack of a role model who can enable them to explore their masculinity with confidence. My own research, based on a number of interviews with men, shows the impact of a lack of fathering, even on adult men.[21] It also shows that men who leave the home do suffer a loss of relationship with their children, even if they have frequent access to them. The encouragement of fatherhood is therefore a key element in the rebuilding of family life.

> The growth of male irresponsibility then reinforces the female drive for independence: even if a girl wanted to grow up to be a dependent homemaker today, she would be ill-advised not to equip herself with job skills, given that her marriage partner is more likely than not to either end up abandoning her and her children, or to have difficulties providing a family income. When these tendencies towards greater independence

on the part of both men and women are reinforced by a general western culture that celebrates individualism, and by a specifically American culture that denigrates the importance of virtually all inherited social duties and obligations, it is easy to see why the United States ends up with a serious degree of family breakdown and declining levels of social capital.[22]

This change in reproductive technology is a good example of the unintended consequences of technological change, which we shall discuss in chapter 7. For women, access to reliable contraception is an important step to freedom and control. It is not possible to disinvent that technology so that it cannot be part of any future economic or social change. It is part of the mosaic of globalization, technological change and cultural attitudes that has brought about an entirely different society. As we have seen, the pressures of the workplace and the often rigid structures of employment have contributed to that change in society as well. Some men and women are thriving on these new freedoms, exploring new working opportunities and enjoying relationships without the earlier trappings, but all is not well. If we are to have healthy families again, they cannot based on an enforced exchange of fertility for economic resources, as was the case before the advent of the Pill. Any change will depend on *recognition of* and *reflection about* the negative consequences of our life together at the moment.

It may be worth adding to the picture with some recent statistics. Traditionally, family life was based on marriage: a permanent, public and, when possible, procreative bond between a man and a woman. Now that institution has, for many, been replaced by cohabitation, in which a man and a woman live together without getting married. In Britain there are an estimated three million people cohabiting at any one time. According to the government's *General Household Survey*, one young adult in four has had a failed live-in relationship. About 23% of men and women aged 25–34 have cohabited in a relationship that has not led to marriage. Nine per cent of men and 6% of women have had two or more such relationships. Twelve per cent of all adults aged 16–59 are currently cohabiting. Fewer than half of marriages now involve couples who have not been living together. The average period of cohabitation is two years.[23]

Just as these figures were published, a European study[24] showed that Britain has the highest number of women in western Europe who are bringing up children without a live-in partner, and described this increase as 'striking'. Fifteen per cent of British women giving birth to a first child do so without having a partner, compared to 9% in France and 6% in Sweden.

It also showed that couples who marry before having a child are consistently more likely to stay together than those who have a baby while cohabiting. Thirty-eight per cent of births in England and Wales were outside marriage, compared with 26% ten years earlier, although more than 60% were registered by two parents giving the same address. (In Scandinavian countries, the majority of babies are born outside marriage.) Ninety-two per cent of British couples who married before they had children stayed together for at least five years, compared to 48% of couples who were cohabiting before having children. The proportion of the adult population which is married is projected to fall below half by 2005.

One other trend is worth noting briefly. In his report *Britain Towards 2010*,[25] Professor Richard Scase predicted that by 2010 single-person households will be the predominant household type, accounting for almost 40% of all households. His prediction is that women will enjoy this and will have an active and varied social life, whereas men will feel isolated, depressed and wedded to their videos, televisions and computers.

These trends show the impact of increased individualism on family life. The concepts of freedom of choice and of individual rights have, together, changed family life out of all recognition. Partnerships between men and women are no longer covenantal, as in a Christian view of marriage, but neither are they really contractual. Essentially they are consensual: a matter of agreement between two parties which can be broken either by mutual consent or by one person walking away from the relationship.

The downside of this is that we are, at the same time, becoming an increasingly isolated society. Many of us struggle with our family commitments without much help, unless we buy it in. Of course, those who are living on low incomes cannot get such help. The increasing demands of working life mean that we are stressed, and rest is at a premium. The pressures of unemployment or under-employment can also lead to stress or depression. A high number of people, who were led to believe that freedom of choice extended to rejecting 'the constraints of marriage' in favour of 'the freedom of cohabitation', have experienced the breakdown of that relationship. This does not mean that all is well with the state of marriage; after all, two out of five marriages end in divorce in the UK. What it does mean is that our current perspective on family life is distorted. Whatever model of family life we have, it is breaking down.

As the family breaks down, society breaks down. Perhaps it is worth reminding ourselves here of one of the key themes discussed at the beginning of this chapter, when we considered a Christian perspective on gender. If it is the case that men and women are walking away from one another, they themselves are becoming fractured as people, since to be human is to be a person in community. The idea of the autonomous self does not allow us to admit to our need for the 'other' and to the knowledge that we are complete only when we are together. It does not allow any sense of dependency on God, nor does it lay the foundations for the dignity and security which come from recognizing one another as made in the image of God. Once these bonds are broken, a self-reinforcing spiral of destruction develops as fear of rejection breeds unwillingness to commit oneself to the other. A one-way dependence of the woman on the man was never a Christian norm.

What is the emerging model of the family? In many cases the absence of a father means that the family consists of mother, child and welfare state. Lionel Tiger calls this a 'bureaugamy'. But the welfare state is increasingly under strain, and politics is changing fast under the impact of globalization. Politics is about the shape of the rapidly changing communities we now we live in, and is the subject of the next chapter.

6
Living in a political community

By the end of the twentieth century, the collapse of communism as a power, the changing role of the nation-state, globalization and its implications for the nature of warfare all showed that the world was changing dramatically. The fall of the Berlin Wall in 1989 signified those changes in a remarkable way. Communism collapsed, not because of military defeat, but because the system was no longer workable. Many assumed that capitalism was now the model for the former communist world to follow. It seemed to have some success in countries such as Hungary, but in others, such as Russia and the Ukraine, the impact of the collapse and the consequent overreaction, which led to ill-advised reforms, was disastrous. Many suffered hunger and poverty as a result.

Communism had shaped a culture entirely different from that of capitalism. Into the vacuum it left surged two opposing forces. One is organized crime, which is reputed to control up to 40% of the Russian economy. Even if this figure is inflated, it is the case that the black market is out of control and criminal behaviour is rising. But the second force is having a completely opposite impact on the culture. In the old Soviet Union, religious revival has filled the vacuum left by ideology. The rise of religion shows that people cannot live by reason alone. Western capitalism calls consumers to act in their own self-interest, but it is impossible to develop a free society without first embracing ethics and a restoration of personal identity. Religion, rather than political ideology, can provide such foundations for a free society. As we shall see, the question whether religion is the foundation for a civil society or just one element in it is being eagerly discussed at the moment. The answer is crucial for the development of Eastern Europe.

The West also was left with a vacuum. Its foreign policy had been formed around the existence of an adversary, or at least of an alternative to capitalism. Everything had to be reassessed, from the existence of nuclear weapons to the way politics, economics and history were taught. For the moment at least, the old ideology had ended. Even without communism, politics had been about political choices described as either left-wing or right-wing. As this distinction also waned, political life drifted towards centrism and pragmatism without any coherent basis for doing so. Talk of a 'Third Way' foundered without an ideology to explain its essence other than that it was a mix of those policies and ideas formerly described as left-wing or right-wing. Policy was judged, not by the extent to which it conformed to some pre-existing ideology, but by its effectiveness in achieving some stated goal.

As free markets became the context for both internal and international trade, welfare capitalism came under pressure. Countries such as the United States and Britain had rapidly ageing populations. Was it possible to cope with the demands this would make on the state? Perhaps the size of the state would be determined by the size of the ageing population. Traditional policy tensions still existed, such as the trade-off between low taxation and the state funding of health, education and other public services. But even the British Labour Party, traditionally left-wing, made a commitment to lower direct taxation as part of their economic policy when they came to power in 1997. The ideological debate of the twentieth century had focused on how much individual freedom should be given up in order to enjoy public services as a community. The measure of this was the size of the tax burden people were willing to bear. The language of the Right was economic freedom, and that of the Left was economic equality. In previous ages the debates had been more about maximizing national power and military capacity, but the Empire had gone and economic competition had replaced imperial pretensions.

The issue of the shape of Europe itself became part of the new agenda. The formation of the Common Market and its evolution into the European Union, the single market and eventually the single currency all became measures of greater co-operation between

European nations. The idea that in time the EU will turn into the Federal States of Europe is frequently debated. This is resisted by Britain, which sees the unifying of continental Europe as, in some way, a threat to its own identity. One indication of this was the hearing many gave to the Conservative Party when it focused British suspicions about Europe in a campaign to retain sterling instead of adopting the euro as its currency. Here was example of the politics of national identity, which had become an important theme throughout the world as the twenty-first century approached.

At the same time, it became apparent that politics itself was not high on the agenda of western societies. The turnout at elections was low and the reputation of politicians was diminished by moral and financial scandals. Political parties did not cope well with changes in culture. People seem to see single-issue groups such a Greenpeace or Amnesty International as representing their views more effectively than any political party. In Britain, the Royal Society for the Protection of Birds has more members than all the political parties combined. Younger people are less likely to vote, to join a party or to become party-politically active. Under-25s are four times less likely to register on the Electoral Roll than any other group. In general, the young are less active in political parties than the old, the poor less than the rich, women less than men and ethnic minorities less than the white majority.[1]

> Political disconnection also leads to broad social disconnection: just 49% of 18–34 year olds say they would be willing to sacrifice some individual freedom in the public interest compared to 61.5% of 35–54 year olds. Over a third of 18–24 year olds take pride being outside the system. But they are nevertheless concerned about many issues: environment, AIDS, jobs and above all animals.[2]

Party manifestos often seem like bundles of seemingly unrelated policies, and in voting for a party one has to vote for the whole bundle whether one agrees with all the policies or not. Will the party keep its promises anyway? The twin revolution of global markets and global information technologies challenges the claims of governments to have access to superior information on many issues. Presumably, as Friedrich Hayek often asserted, this means that there is no reason why governments should be any better at making decisions than the individual.[3]

Citizenship is traditionally the foundation of national and political identity. The displacement of citizenship by self-interested individualism has therefore had a fragmenting effect on national identity. Although I may know what I believe in as an individual, the question is whether we know what we believe in as a community. Perhaps this is because so many of the symbols of citizenship, such as the monarchy, the place of Britain in the world, our pride in our history and our respect for our institutions, have been replaced by a sense of doubt about whether these things appropriately express a modern nation. The very idea of national pride seems to some to be oppressive, not only in our multicultural society, but also internationally in a postmodern world where all cultures are meant to be equal. Civil society has always seen these institutions as an important part of social cohesion, and has regarded their loss as contributing to the crisis of identity we are currently experiencing. National pride is now expressed through activities such as sport, which does not carry connotations of cultural superiority.

Commenting on these issues, Dr Jonathan Sacks, the Chief Rabbi, wrote:

> I sense among the young people I meet in schools and youth groups something I have not met with before: cynicism and absence of hope, as if, every political alternative having been tried and failed, expectation of things getting better is bound to be disappointed ... A decade of individualism has taken a heavy toll of the traditions by which our collective identity was given shape. It would be hard today to describe what being British is, in any terms other than nostalgia for a long-vanished past.[4]

The politics of culture

British politician Chris Patten, Governor of Hong Kong before its handover to China, and now a European Commissioner, has said,

> I am increasingly obsessed with ... the problem of the underclass, which I believe we cannot ignore. In the past it has usually been true that when a community gets better off, everyone gets better off. But that has stopped happening. People with skills get better off, people with no skills get left behind. We have a bigger and bigger underclass because the jobs they used to do are now being done in Guangdong province and in East Asia generally ... I find myself in complete agreement with somebody like Tony Blair and his stress on social cohesion and community values.[5]

The privatization of our lives has led to the fracturing of community values. The new agenda for politics has centred on the word 'community', which is another way of talking about identity in a time when it is under threat. We are nostalgic for our sense of belonging. We imagine that there were golden ages in the past when life was simpler, friendlier and somehow on a more human scale than it is now. What we do know now is that politics is not about tinkering with the tools of economic management or the fostering of ideology. Governments can sustain only that political life that arises out of the commitments of people themselves. Politicians are asking questions about culture and community values as never before.

In an article on the relationship between government and culture, researcher Perri 6 writes:

> The wider culture is now the centre of the agenda for government reform, because we now know from the findings of a wide range of recent research that culture is perhaps the most important determinant of a combination of long-run economic success and social cohesion. The mistake of both statist Left and laissez-faire Right was to ignore this fact. In the long run, the societies that show the greatest economic dynamism and viable social cohesion are the ones where a culture of high trust enables individuals to create organizations readily, to take personal responsibility but also to sustain long-term co-operative relations in trading with and employing people who are strangers to them.[6]

Civil society depends on certain values being in place, without which no community can survive, or at least be healthy. Virtues such as trust, honesty and reciprocity are at the heart of all human relationships. Since the ideological debate about freedom and equality has been put to one side in favour of centrism and pragmatism, the attention of politicians is turning to the relationship between freedom and order and the politics of culture. How do people form the relationships that will lead to a healthy society? It is important that trust and honesty are not just practised within the family but that they spill out into the wider society, in order that strangers can co-operate in the setting up of companies and the forming of voluntary associations, which bring people together in relationships of high trust. Without the extension of trust to the wider society, society cannot grow.

To be human is to be in relationship with God and with others. If there is no God, the question is whether being a social animal is sufficient spontaneously to form the bonds necessary to build healthy communities. If it is sufficient, religion, although it may be helpful as a social influence, is not necessary, since people will act honestly or in a trustworthy way because it is in their best interests to do so. Since acting as if freedom has no limits means that we quickly find ourselves adversely affected by the selfish behaviour of others, we shall create rules that will place moral constraints on individual choices. We find ourselves treating others as we would like to be treated ourselves. Of course, there will be crime and other forms of deviance, but rules will be formed and punishments devised to ensure that such behaviour is seen to be unacceptable. Such prohibitions will entail the development of hierarchies with power to enforce them.

Families and formal education are important in shaping such values and in transmitting them throughout society. Children learn within families, not only by imitating their parents' behaviour but also by heeding their advice as to what is acceptable in the wider society. Schools cannot cope with children who have not had those lessons inculcated in them from birth. They cannot replace the family and, if civil society works against the family, either by denying its importance or by undermining it, as has recently been the case in the West, it reaps the consequences of this in the wider society.

From a liberal perspective then, people will create the rules of behaviour without needing God to tell them what those rules are, or even without legislators to formalize them, since people know what is in their best interests. Economist Norman Barry comments:

> It is not understood enough that the practice of trade itself generates those capacities of honesty and trust that the market needs. We do not have to know each other to follow these rules, least of all need we share the same religion or belong to the same race; we simply have to be regular participants in the practice of dealing and trading. We in effect play repeated games and this enables us to identify cheats, liars and non-cooperators ... moral rules are simple *conventions* and though they are often sanctioned by a religion, which gives them a moral gloss that encourages obedience, their rationale is strictly human.[7]

On this view, the useful thing about religion is that it tends to uphold those moral values that contribute to the success of the market. It is because these general morals of the market are compatible with the moral codes of all religions, that the market is such a widespread instrument of global wealth creation. In other words, one does not need to believe in the 'religious' element of religion to appreciate its importance for the market (or indeed for civil society), but only in its most basic moral commitments. For Barry, this morality has to be 'minimalist'. If markets are required to serve particular visions of social morality, they will not work properly.

If religion is not the most important foundation for civil society, it is argued, what matters is that people observe that minimal morality required for economic efficiency. Whatever the *intentions* people have, what *matters* is their behaviour. A company may have a reputation for honesty, not because its directors are altruistic, but because the company performs better as a result. People may keep their commitments because their business contacts are more likely to keep their commitments as a result. Yet competition and co-operation continuously interact with each other and are sometimes difficult to separate. The market behaviour that may cause self-interest to spill over into the community, so that people become greedy, may also be the source of new moral values as people realize

Living in a political community   111

that contracts have to be maintained, deadlines kept, quality assured and work conditions improved.

Advocates of this position, such as Francis Fukuyama, realize that it is impossible to ignore the importance of religion in contributing to the existence of those moral values which are the building-blocks of civil society. Religion is often said to be the cause of violence between people rather than the glue that holds them together. But the twentieth century, the most secular of all centuries, was the most bloody and violent of them all. In the long term, the rise of religion has been essential in engendering those values that have changed society. It is not only that Christianity has been the source of important ideas such as the concept of universal human rights. The formation of so many voluntary associations, such as Sunday schools or the YMCA, especially in the nineteenth century, enabled communities to develop patterns of behaviour that curbed antisocial problems such as drunkenness, gambling and crime. The abolition of slavery and the Factory Acts were a direct result of Christian social action. The rise of Victorian England, so often dismissed as oppressive and prudish, saw remarkable growth in the virtues and values that strengthen civil society. In examining the global religious resurgence at the end of the twentieth century, Samuel Huntington wrote:

> ... the religious resurgence throughout the world is a reaction against secularism, moral relativism and self-indulgence, and a reaffirmation of the values of order, discipline, work, mutual help and human solidarity. Religious groups meet social needs left unattended by state bureaucracy. These include the provision of medical and hospital services, kindergartens and schools, care for the elderly, prompt relief after natural and other catastrophes and welfare support during periods of economic deprivation. The breakdown of order and civilised societies are filled by religious and often fundamentalist groups.[8]

Within the argument we have been considering so far, the importance of religion does not necessarily entail the existence of God. All that can be claimed is that the religious imagination is an important generator of moral values. In other words, God is there because we need him to be there. For example, many people who no longer attend church want to send their own children to church. They do this for many reasons, but often because they see the church as a 'good influence'; a partner with them as parents in bringing up their children.[9]

The idea that complete social decline was inevitable because morality was generated solely by religious commitment implied that, once religious belief was dead and gone, society would irrevocably break up. But this is wrong on two counts. First, the moral values of a culture are not solely dependent on religious belief, even though this is extremely important. From a theological standpoint, all of us are made in the image of God whether we are religious or not. Secondly, despite statistics which assert that church attendance is declining in some areas, religion continues to be a vital part of western culture. Culture has not become completely secularized in the way it was once thought to have done, and in the 1990s religion was back on the agenda.

The liberal argument about the generation of 'social capital' can afford to be optimistic because it sees people as always returning to the generation of those values that society needs in order to function as a healthy community. Historically, there have been far worse periods than today in terms of deviance and antisocial behaviour. Although some of those were transformed by religious renewal, such as the Weslyan revival, this was not always the case. Liberals take heart from this, believing in the importance of the spontaneous generation of moral constraints. The threat to these was, until recently, thought to be socialism. In its purest form it removed from people the necessity of developing those proactive patterns of behaviour that maintain a free society. The collapse of communism and the rise of consumerism, however, have focused the debate on another interesting issue. Could it be that the unfettered market becomes the enemy of the free society on which it depends?

There is a long tradition of disagreement with the liberal views I have discussed above. From this contrary perspective, the moral values necessary for a healthy society are generated not by the market but outside it. These values are primarily religious, and are derived from a tradition that gives individuals dignity and respect because they are made in the image and likeness of God. For instance, in his recent study on the wealth and poverty of nations, David Landes examines the reasons for the superior wealth creation of Europe and North America. He finds these in Judeo-Christianity. Its respect for manual labour, its subordination of labour to humanity and its sense of time as linear, and the importance it gives to the market, to creativity and innovation and to private-property rights all combine to form a unique framework for the development of a market economy.[10]

Religion has thus been an important element in the development of capitalism itself. Judaism has never been at odds with business life, but has always encouraged the creation of wealth, the skills of entrepreneurship and the notion of the stewardship of resources. (Puritanism similarly encouraged hard work and thrift as objects of divine blessing.) In the 1998 Hayek Memorial Lecture, Jonathan Sacks examined the relationship between morality, markets and the heritage of Judaism. He argued that Judaism has always been pro-market. Though it has a real concern for poverty, he argues, this is not solved within Judaism by formal redistribution of wealth but by ensuring that each person has access to work through which individuals can make their own living. The Jewish picture of *shalom* as each man 'sitting under his own fig tree'[11] is a picture of a man who has dignity because he is earning his own living and is content with what he has.

Yet Dr Sacks' concern is that free markets undermine society. The distinctive institutions on which society rests and which, he argues, are the heritage of Judaism, come from outside the market. These are the Sabbath, marriage and the family, publicly funded education, ownership as trusteeship and the Jewish tradition of the law. These are not based on economic decision-making:

> ... they were ways in which Judaism, in effect, said to the market: thus far and no further. There are realms into which you may not intrude. The concept of the holy is precisely the domain in which the worth of things is not judged by their market price or economic value.[12]

Anti-market rhetoric, until recently, identified the one who used it as a socialist. Now there is confusion as to what position such a person might hold. There is even more confusion when a critic of the market comes from a long pro-market tradition and still acknowledges the extraordinary power for good that the market has exercised in human history. But the position adopted by Dr Sacks is central to an understanding of a Christian critique of the market and of the nature of civil society. It is impossible for Judeo-Christian traditions to be satisfied with a libertarian view of civil society or of the market economy precisely because such a position usually regards humanity solely as a social animal. But that is not enough. Humanity is a divine creation. We cannot escape that fact, nor can we divorce it from our moral behaviour. As at so many turning-points in this book, we cannot be satisfied with human reason when we believe in divine revelation. Any argument for the existence of those institutions ordained by God that bases them on human reason must be rejected as inadequate.

The market should restrict itself, then, to the domain in which it has something to offer us, and economics should restrict itself to the activity it best explains: the exchange of goods and services. The Chief Rabbi continues:

> ... it is not my case to oppose the market. As, I argued, the Judaic tradition holds the market and its attendant virtues in high regard. My case is different. It can be stated thus. *Ideas and institutions that have great benefit in their own domain have disastrous consequences when they are applied to another domain.* Religion has great virtues in ordering communities. It has dire results when employed to govern states. Scientific method is supreme in explaining natural phenomena. It is catastrophic when used to prescribe human behaviour. Markets are the best way we know of structuring exchanges – goods to be bought and sold. They are far from the best way of ordering relationships or preserving goods whose value is not identical with their price.[13]

It may be enough for Judaism to claim that being pro-market under certain constraints accurately represents its tradition, but this is not so for the Christian tradition. As we have already seen, Jesus starkly contrasted God and Money (Mammon), and this has led to continuous debate over the last 2,000 years about how to live out his teaching. Christians have found it difficult to reconcile the demands of Christian teaching with market behaviour. Pursuing personal gain does not seem to be a part of the teaching of Jesus. Samuel Brittan, the economist and financial journalist, in an essay entitled 'Two cheers for self-interest', pointed out that

> Christ's parables are full of sayings about the folly of pursuing wealth. 'Go thy way,' said Jesus to a man who asked what he should do to inherit eternal life: 'Sell whatever thou hast, and give to the poor, and thou shalt have treasure in heaven.' He did not say: 'Make a fortune, float the company and give the proceeds to famine relief.' Such a rationalisation could perhaps be supported by the Old Testament but scarcely by the New. Most attempts to show the compatibility of Adam Smith economics and the Bible lean heavily on the Old Testament and on sophisticated interpretation of the New, and warn against liberal quotation of the latter. What could be more opposed to conventional rational behaviour (in either a market or a planned economy) than 'Take no thought for the morrow, for the morrow shall take thought for the things of itself. Sufficient unto the day is the evil thereof'?[14]

Yet Jesus taught that God knew that people needed food, drink and clothing, and he also sent his disciples to buy bread. We cannot, however, escape the suspicion Christianity has towards market capitalism. Christianity is concerned, as we saw in the discussion of consumerism in chapter 4, that the pursuit of wealth will change the spiritual attitude of the individual, making it impossible for him or her to accept the teaching of Christ. It is also concerned about the standard of living of people in the community, since, if some have more than they need, it may be at the expense of those who are poor. Such thinking extends to global equity. Christians have always been troubled about a world in which so many people are destitute. Despite the market's ideological rationale for this inequality, there seems to be a fundamental injustice about it. The apostle Paul, writing about the poverty of the Jerusalem church, invites the Corinthian church to give so that each might have enough.[15] It is not, he says, that he wants them to become poor and the others rich, but that they should give out of their excess so that the Jerusalem Christians may have what they need. The principle of 'enough', combined with a focus on the kingdom of God rather than on material gain, is at the heart of living out the teaching of Jesus. Even when we think we are living like this, his teaching is so uncompromising that its challenge to self-interested living never wanes.

What about market behaviour, then? If we all acted in an altruistic way in the market-place, disaster would result. If the factories gave away their goods, they would not be able to pay wages. If I insisted on giving you my house instead of selling it to you, I would be penniless and on the streets. Markets are the best way of exchanging goods and services. They co-ordinate the actions of millions of people, gather information about our tastes and preferences so that producers can respond creatively to them, and stimulate technological development. They do this as much for the street trader in Delhi as for the multinational based in New York. Perhaps what is happening in the market is that people who act in altruistic and loving ways in the rest of their lives know that they must act as if they were self-interested in order to get what they want in the market-place. It does not mean that they are greedy. All it means is that such activity enables the market to function properly. There is a problem with this, though: people do not confine their pursuit of self-interest to what they need, but often make self-interest a goal in itself. The market does not discriminate between the two kinds of behaviour. Those who are greedy gain their rewards just like those who have more modest requirements. The psalmists frequently question why wicked men prosper when doing so seems so unfair.[16] Those who lose out in the market-place are those who bring nothing to it. You cannot receive from the market unless you have either money or something to sell. Jesus said, 'You will always have the poor among you.'[17]

John Stott once suggested that the Christian response to these issues was to live according to three principles: simplicity, generosity and contentment.[18] Simplicity helps us to contain our greed within a modest lifestyle. Contentment equips us to resist the fallacious lure of advertising. Generosity enables us to go some way towards meeting the needs of those who are poor. Living by these principles demonstrates that there is another way of living – according to the kingdom of God.

False morality

As we shall see in the next chapter, both markets and technology are essentially distributors of information. To be constructive, that information needs to be limited to the sphere of activity for which it is designed. Both market information and technical information do, in a time of rapid technological change and of economic growth, have a tendency to exploit any opportunity that yields a return. The more a society becomes technological, the further its values become the subject of economic calculus rather than being seen as representing those virtues and values that are generated by religious life. In chapter 3 I wrote of the way our society generates spurious values that appear to be moral values but are capable of manipulation by the market.

In a previous book[19] I described in more detail the way this works within markets. Terms such as 'cost-effective' or 'need' seem to represent moral values against which it is difficult to argue. The same is true of words such as 'choice', 'tolerance' and 'discrimination' in political discourse. But these are not moral words in and of themselves; they need to be qualified by adjectives with moral content. One notorious word is 'uneconomic'. The economist and philosopher Fritz Schumacher drew attention to the use of this word in his book *Small is Beautiful*. The passage has been quoted extensively, but it is worth reminding ourselves of it:

> In the current vocabulary of condemnation there are few words that are as final and conclusive as "uneconomic'. If an activity has been branded as uneconomic, its right to existence is not merely questioned but fundamentally denied. Anything that is found to be an impediment to economic growth is a shameful thing, and if people cling to it they are thought of as either saboteurs or fools. Call a thing immoral or ugly, soul destroying or a degradation of man, a peril to the peace of the world or to the well-being of future generations,

so long as you have not shown it to be 'uneconomic' you have not really questioned its right to exist, grow or prosper.[20]

Both economic markets and civil society, then, depend on certain values, virtues and habits of behaviour which, if they are not present, will lead to their breakdown. The absence of honesty will lead to high costs incurred by policing the market. Morality is cost-effective! In asking where these values come from, however, we cannot be satisfied with the idea that those who take part in market transactions generate them. They arise from the fact that we are made in the image of God, and, historically, from the Judeo-Christian tradition which has come down to us over many hundreds of years. If this tradition is discarded, market behaviour, especially in a technological age, will spill out of its appropriate confines, which are defined by institutions given by God. If those institutions are abandoned, the consumerism that results begins to destroy the human spirit, and to lay waste human communities by always addressing people as individuals.

The existence and the working of both free markets and democracy depend on a particular type of moral commitment. It is a commitment, not to ideology but to one another, not to policy but to the maintenance of life in community. This commitment to trust and emphasis on the community has focused the political debate on to the nature of community and the importance of its culture.

Community and belonging

In an interview conducted in 1995, Tony Blair commented:

> Where my political and personal beliefs completely coincide is the notion that people are members of a community and society, not simply individuals, isolated and alone ... You are what you are in part because of others, and you cannot divorce the individual from the surrounding society. Indeed socialism started off as a theory about society, and I think that is very clear not just in Christian teaching but in Old Testament teaching as well. The idea of the individual and their place in society is to me (apart from the spiritual

dimension) the distinguishing philosophical feature of the Christian religion and it just happens to be the same as my political belief.[21]

In the 1990s the idea of 'communitarianism' started a debate that was energized by the recognition that a new paradigm was needed for political life. Initially, it focused on the work of American thinker Amitai Etzioni and philosopher David Selbourne. Interestingly, both are from a Jewish background. Etzioni's work, in particular, had a widespread impact on the thinking of political leaders during the 1990s.

The idea is simple. The modern world has emphasized rights at the expense of responsibilities or duties, leaving us with individuals and groups who compete with one another as they claim their various rights. Who is responsible for meeting these claims? If someone has a 'right' (rather than just a 'want'), someone else must have a corresponding obligation to meet the claim. But we live in a culture of 'dutiless rights', in which people want what they believe is theirs but are not willing to take on board their own responsibilities to others. Etzioni cites young people in America who would wish to be tried by a jury of their peers but are unwilling to do jury service themselves. Here is a breakdown of the reciprocity that is essential to the working of civil society.

Communitarians emphasize that in order to be 'free', people need to be members of a community. This community backs them up against encroachment by the state, and sustains morality by drawing on personal, family and community relationships, as distinct from coercion by the state.[22]

For Etzioni, morality is a community affair. Conscience is not a sufficient moral guide. He recognizes that society cannot function properly if its citizens do not behave morally. Community is like a set of Russian dolls. From the family outwards to the European Union, each level of society must act morally if the next is to have a chance to do so. If there is something wrong with families, there may well be something wrong with democracy as a whole. If we are to be 'multiple citizens', as suggested in chapter 2, we must recognize that each of the domains to which we belong is a moral one.

At the local level, however, people help each other to live morally (in this view) by personal reproof or encouragement of one another on issues such as litter-dropping, stopping at red lights or keeping our lawn mown. Too many people are frightened to say anything on such matters, afraid of being thought puritanical, authoritarian or self-righteous. Etzioni's book *The Spirit of Community* suggests that the communitarian approach cuts across the conventional political agenda by enabling communities to reflect on issues such as parenting and divorce and their impact on the family. Indeed, families are the first line in a communitarian transformation of society, with schools next and then wider local and national communities. In communitarianism we cross the divide from political economy to the politics of culture.

Communitarianism sets great store by the formation of mediating structures, especially voluntary groups in which people are encouraged to work together for common community causes and to help each other to formulate clear moral guidelines for doing so. It is essentially a relational way of solving our problems rather than relying on regulation and coercion from the state. It links moral behaviour with the possibility of reducing the size of government, since moral behaviour would reduce the need for public expenditure on law enforcement.

Like Etzioni, David Selbourne stresses the problem of dutiless rights:

> The old socialism is dead; the new social-ism, neither of the 'left' nor 'right' but transcending both and resting upon the principle of duty, is waiting to be born. The overthrow and fall of old socialism, with its dogmas, servitudes to class, party and state, and ... recoil from the principle of duty, especially as it applies to the citizen's obligations to himself, his familiars, and to the civic order in the form of nation, has opened the way to a new social-ism of the civic bond.[23]

We owe duty not to dogma or to ideology but to one another. The question of human motivation is taken seriously for once. We are not reduced to either self-interest or some kind of altruism; rather, the way we operate together as a community is considered important. Politics, in this view, is not about the means and ends of policy but about the processes and relationships of the people. This means that the discussion in chapter 5 about the nature of the relationship between men and women, and about our changing perspectives on our own identity, become integral to our political life.

Two prospects are worth mentioning as a response to this focus on the community. The first is the future of volunteering. There has been an increased interest in volunteering in recent years, precisely because the voluntary sector, which has always made a notable contribution to community life, has achieved national significance.

The second concerns the role of faith communities (or faith-based organizations, as they are sometimes called). One of the ways in which they work out their faith is in caring for the poor, the elderly and others in need. Many of their projects have become increasingly sophisticated in recent years, and they now supply a considerable amount of social care outside the state sector. Although, in many cases, such projects receive some government finance, the convergence of volunteering and the activities of faith communities constitutes an important outworking of the politics of community.

Political parties, both in the UK and in the US, are now emphasizing the importance of faith communities. Although this looks like a helpful recognition of the work such communities undertake, it risks politicizing their work. Faith communities are part of an agenda that emphasizes a 'bottom-up' approach to social need. A political 'takeover' would harm their work and undermine the relationship between faith and action on which their vision is based. If the work of faith communities and of volunteers were to be seen as creating space for the 'rolling back of the welfare state', this would be a major disaster in the eyes of those who work in such programmes. For all the deficiencies of the welfare state, its principles and those of faith communities are similar in that both are trying to meet the needs of those who are socially excluded.

Freedom and order

How do we find a balance between individual interests and the common good? If a society strays too far away from that balance, it needs to be brought back. We want to offer people the respect and dignity they are due, since we are all made in the image of God.

Communitarianism attempts to balance freedom and order. It sees the relationship between them as a measuring-rod by which any society can be assessed. Thus Iran is a society of excessive order, and the United States one of excessive liberty. While both culture and historical context change, the measuring-rod does not. The balance between freedom and equality is more difficult, in Etzioni's view, because 'equality is a more elusive concept'.[24] It is possible to reduce inequality, but not to achieve equality, especially if it is defined in economic terms. Etzioni cites his experience of life in a kibbutz as evidence of a situation where equality was always breaking down, even though it was the primary goal of that small community. The kind of equality that is important is our equal moral worth, which is essential if the idea of rights is to have any meaning.

In his view, the values that guide us as a society are, as the American Declaration of Independence puts it, self-evident truths. They are not contractual or consensual; they are *a priori*, or, in Etzioni's words, 'they speak to us'. There is room for debate about these values and how they should be applied, but they are fundamental to all human life. Etzioni argues that these values can be enhanced by heeding the moral voice in all of us. If that were to happen, society would improve without sacrificing either freedom or order. ('You can have your cake and eat it.') He cites organ donation as an example of the options open to a society. The state can coerce by legislation that presumes consent, as in Singapore, or permit a free market in which organs are bought and sold, as libertarians advocate. The communitarian approach would be to suggest that to donate organs is a civic duty, but one that individuals can avoid without sanctions if they wish to do so.

In *The New Golden Rule*, Etzioni argues that a society should hesitate to pass more laws unless they express its moral voice. First, a public debate is needed. Then legislators, having listened to it, should frame a law which people have already agreed to keep. In other words, moral commitments reduce the need for legislation, and legislation that reflects the moral voice will be heeded. Consensus is important when policies are framed, as long as they do not affect certain basic commitments such as those that might be enshrined in a Bill of Rights. Consensus is not perfect, but it is better than nothing.

For Etzioni, fundamentalism is a major problem facing society. In Israel, he says, 'they are holding peace hostage'. Nevertheless, the divide in society is not between those who believe that the moral voice is based on reason and those who believe it comes from divine revelation, but between those two groups on the one hand, and on the other those who are 'basically amoral' or who see only 'the market-place or self-interest and celebrate that'.

> I wouldn't for a second say that communitarianism exhausts all moral values and there's nothing to be added: there is room for more morality and commitments. You can talk about community in a secular sense; I am much more interested in the notion of caring for others. But it is not that I have to care about the poor or the sick or the vulnerable or the least among us on the basis of one-to-one. The idea is basically to make them members of our community, to count them as full moral people – I mean they are all made in God's image – and share and reach out to them. Now, that certainly is very Christian as far as I know (I'm not an expert on Christianity). It is certainly very communitarian.[24]

This emphasis on personal responsibility as well as on rights is important for Christians. Its importance is well illustrated when we consider the nature of the welfare system that we are struggling to sustain. The problem the welfare state faces is that the language of rights has become impoverished. So many claims are made on the state that the benefits that can be claimed by right are reduced to what governments can provide. Yet politicians can provide very little apart from economic help and social services. This demonstrates the reductionist impact of the language of economics on modern politics. People need more than rights-goods if they are to thrive as well as survive. Our goal as communities and as a civil society should be human flourishing rather than mere survival. Love, respect and dignity are crucial to our experience of what it means to be human. They go beyond the moral values needed simply to preserve the civic order. It is not true to say that love and respect (or their opposites) do not matter to those receiving benefits from the state. Nor should love and respect demand anything in return. The

Good Samaritan acted without any reciprocal exchange, and genuine love for others does the same. Politics rarely talks of love, believing that if people have their basic physical needs met, their emotional needs also will be met in some way.

Michael Ignatief wrote in his book *The Needs of Strangers*:

> Giving the aged poor their pension and providing them with medical care may be a necessary condition for their self-respect and their dignity, but it is not a sufficient condition. It is the manner of the giving that counts and the moral basis on which it is given: whether strangers at my door get their stories listened to by the social worker, whether the ambulance man takes care not to jostle them when they are taken down the steep stairs of their apartment building, whether a nurse sits with them in the hospital when they are frightened and alone. Respect and dignity are conferred by gestures such as these. They are gestures too much a matter of human art to be made a consistent matter of administrative routine.[25]

There is the kind of respect that considers all people as the same, with the same needs for warmth, food, shelter and so on. Justice demands that there should be no discrimination against anybody but that all should be treated equally. Systems are good at delivering this kind of respect: 'tick the box' and get the goods. But an alternative model of respect assumes that individuals are unique and that we cannot assume anything about them before we have heard their story. This kind of respect cannot be delivered by systems, but only by communities. It takes relationship to respect diversity. As I have commented before, 'no system can deliver love'.[26]

Communities are places where we voluntarily interact with others, where we confer respect, honour and dignity on one another. But heated discussion and disagreement can also occur within the bonds of the commitment to the community. Communities cannot be said to be strong if they do not include these elements within their life.

Communities can form around very different sets of values. After all, both the Hezbollah and the Real IRA are communities. Where can we derive the values to sustain community life and prevent it from becoming coercive or totalitarian? What view of human nature can provide enough freedom for creativity but enough constraint on evil? Christianity has a great deal to offer any politics that seeks to understand people and communities. It offers a unique basis for such understanding in that it allows for confidence in truth revealed but humility about truth expressed. It views truth as utterly dependent on the transcendent God, yet as understood through the immanence of the incarnation.

Richard Neuhaus relates this to democracy:

> Democracy is the appropriate form of governance in a fallen creation in which no person or institution, including the Church, can infallibly speak for God. Democracy is the necessary expression of humility in which all persons and institutions are held accountable to transcendent purposes imperfectly discerned ... Of course democracy is unsatisfactory. All orders short of the Kingdom of God are unsatisfactory. The discontents of democracy – its provisionality and incompleteness – are the signs of political health. The hunger for a truly satisfying way of putting the world in order is laudable. But that is a hunger for the Kingdom of God, and it is dangerously misplaced when it is invested in the political arena.[27]

An important factor as we work our way forward as a society is the kind of openness to the voices of others that refuses to deify our own perspective, but is content to argue for it openly. Paradoxically, the strength of a free society is that it is always fragile. It has to enable voices to be raised within it which constantly threaten to take it over. If a society prevents those voices from being heard, because it is concerned about their threat to it, that society is no longer free. This freedom within the rule of law is finely balanced in a democracy. Those who protested against high fuel taxes in Britain and elsewhere in Europe in the autumn of 2000 disrupted the economy by preventing fuel deliveries and nearly brought it to its knees. They claimed to be exercising their democratic right to protest. Others argued that the proper way to influence government policy was by persuasion. Democracies walk a fine line.

Democracy is necessarily a compromise because all systems short of the kingdom of God are compromises. In acknowledging our imperfect discernment, we avoid the dogmatic certainties of fundamentalism which, in seeking to bring about the kingdom on earth, becomes violent. Belief in the transcendence of God helps us to understand something more about that love and justice which are necessary for the encouragement of others. We also understand something about the source of the hunger that drives all human endeavour. So our restlessness and our frustration are the guardians of our freedom. They are the ever-present witnesses that we long for ideals that cannot be attained, but which should shape the efforts of all those who wield power in our society. From a Christian perspective, it is the kingdom of God that provides the pattern and the model for all political life, and which at the same time acts as the standard by which that life is to be judged. Our freedom depends as much on our admission of imperfect discernment as on those transcendent purposes which have recently been out of focus in contemporary politics.

As soon as we acknowledge that human community is always going to be imperfect and that we ourselves contribute to that imperfection, we have to find ways of dealing with it that are not necessarily legislative. We have to come back to the level of the community. But it is not enough to have community meetings that discuss rules to prevent the dropping of litter. These relationships need demonstrations of love, forgiveness, mercy and respect for difference. This is the language of the kingdom of God, and the development of such bonds between strangers requires an understanding of its importance, not only in the lives of individuals, but also in the life of the state.

It is it at this local level that 'trust' can be renewed.

Despite the importance of the community at the local level, however, it is national government that sets the framework within which we live as communities. Etzioni wants government to legislate after first understanding the moral will of the people. Debates are, of course, vital in a democratic society. But many of the most contentious moral issues, such as abortion, animal rights or homosexuality, are never resolved. This is because moral opinion is so deeply divided, and because of the relativistic climate that deters us from concluding that one side is right and the other wrong. Etzioni's idea that debate confers legitimacy on legislation seems to play into the hands of modern politics, which has become an endless debate. For every position held, there is an opposite, and the debates are interminable. Morality seems to be a poor relation of politics, unable to be decisive in the face of the actions of politicians. Moral arguments, instead of revealing truth, become a way of disagreeing with the positions of others, and therefore part of social discourse, as Oliver O'Donovan has pointed out. As a result, politics becomes autonomous. Why should one position be right and another wrong? How can we possibly decide, in a postmodern world? Moral authority becomes suspect, since it cannot help to resolve anything.

Of course, a government does have authority, and the citizen has a duty to submit to its rule. But placing laws on the statute book which are superfluous, immoral or incapable of enforcement will inevitably undermine its authority. So it is vital that government sees itself as legislating within a moral tradition. One of the duties of government is the maintenance of that tradition which reflects the moral voice of previous generations and which forms the foundation on which civil society rests. Government does not come to every issue as if it were new, seeking the moral voice anew. Rather, it interprets each issue within that tradition. The burden of proof rests with those who seek change. They must argue for the necessity of reform or the introduction of new legislation. Much new legislation will not be a problem, as it will respond to the need for regulation, provision or innovation by applying the well-known rules of engagement between government and people. It is the strength of democracy that even though we may argue against the efficacy of a particular policy, we still pay our taxes which enable such policies to be put into effect. The authority of government continues, even though we may sometimes disagree with some of its policies.

Even more importantly, the government is not only bound to represent truth as expressed in tradition, but is also held accountable to that truth. All good government depends on this double emphasis on truth and accountability. Yet it is that very concept of truth, and therefore of tradition, that our society cannot accept. This produces the vacuum at the heart of contemporary politics and the inability of politicians to appeal to moral authority. When we ask where the authority of government comes from, or what that truth is to which tradition refers and to which governments are accountable, we have to turn to Christian teaching. For it is on the relationship of the state to the kingdom (or kingship of God) that truth, accountability and tradition depend.

The kingship of God

To say that the Bible is a very political book raises the spectre of using the Bible to support political beliefs that are not derived from it, thus lending such views a spurious authority. It may also reinforce fears that politicians or church leaders may use their authority to 'meddle' in each other's affairs, with disastrous consequences. Claiming that the Bible is a political book does not meaning that it is party-political. The Bible focuses on the 'politics of God'. It does so because in its pages God reveals himself as the ultimate ruler – the King of kings. Consequently, one of the main themes of the Bible is the 'kingdom of God', which is crucial for our understanding of God, the church and civil society, including the role of the state.

God has declared how he wants us to live. He gave Israel the Law and the Prophets to enable them to live justly and righteously. Israel was distinctive as a nation because from the outset Yahweh was king. He showed, in the way he dealt with Israel, what it meant to live under divine kingship. This was not some ideal concept that remains an unattainable goal, even though, because of human sin and frailty, it can never be realized through the operation of human institutions. God showed that kingship was expressed not only through holiness but also through mercy. God declared himself to be king of a fallen people, and his kingship was made evident not through abstract rules but through his engagement with the minutiae of Israel's social, economic and cultural life. 'The kingdom of God' is therefore a descriptive term; Israel's culture was distinctive because Yahweh was her king. As Moses says to God, Israel would have lost her distinctiveness if God had not been with his people. [28]

'The kingdom of God' is also prescriptive, indicating how all people made in the image of God should behave towards one another and towards God. Israel could not take it for granted that just because Yahweh was her king her community would retain those elements of his rule that express his holy character. The prophets constantly had to call Israel back to God because her life as a community depended on an active and obedient relationship with God. The formula 'I will ... be your God, and you will be my people',[29] reveals that this relationship between king and people is covenantal. The heart of God's kingship is salvation itself.

God's kingship was revealed not only in the law, which regulated the society and protected the vulnerable, and in God's provision for atonement, but also in Israel's military life. Israel was distinctive in that the deciding factor in many of the wars she fought was not her overwhelming military power, but precisely the opposite. In the story of Gideon, for instance, the presence of God and Gideon's obedience to God are the key factors in what was a decisive victory. Through military victory God 'saved' his people, but the manner in which it occurred emphasized again not only the presence of God with his people, but also the character of God, indicated by his opposition to what the victory destroyed. God's victory through Israel's weakness also affirmed her call to a life that was different from the surrounding nations.

When Israel decided she wanted a human king, like the surrounding nations, God spoke of her request as an act of rejection of his kingly rule. He warned them of the consequences that would distinguish such a rule from his own. The king would use the sons of Israel to drive his chariots and would make some serve under commanders, while others would have to till his land rather than their own. Israel's daughters would become his servants. The king would take the best of the land and its produce and distribute them at his pleasure. In effect, the people would 'become his slaves'. As a result, they would 'cry out' because of the impact of such kingship on their lives.[30] But choosing monarchy would be an irrevocable step; there would be no going back to theocracy. Israel wanted to be like the other nations, and preferred to have a king to lead them into battle rather than to depend on an invisible God.

All these negative characteristics of human rule serve to highlight the fact that God's kingship is merciful and just, and that it affirms both the world and its people. As the redemptive creator, God had been working within human history to bring about his purposes, which are protective rather than exploitative. God's authority had been made known through his actions, but the human king would assume authority by virtue of his office.[31] He was constantly called to recognize that his kingship was to mirror God's kingship, just as the earthly tabernacle mirrored the worship of heaven. Though the compromise was a sad rejection of God's own rule, the human king was still called to be God's representative.

Political authority can exist only if it mirrors the authority God exercises as king. The state must exercise power, it must do right and it must govern within a moral tradition. If it does not, it fails to exercise legitimate authority. Such authority derives from divine providence rather than from what Oliver O'Donovan calls the 'human task of political service'.[32] But the people have a part to play, in that they must acknowledge political authority as such. O'Donovan comments that society proves its political identity in doing so.

No government can claim to be doing what God would do in the circumstances unless all the characteristics that mark God's rule are present. The onus is on the government, by its actions, to show that they are present. But just as the Israelite monarchy was always a compromise compared to the direct rule of God, so is modern government. The fact that we live in a modern or postmodern world does not mean that the tie between God's authority and that of earthly rulers has been broken.

The outworking of God's kingly rule in her society led Israel to worship him for that rule. As O'Donovan comments, the worshipping community is a political community. Worship draws us towards the political, not away from it: 'praise is the final cause of God's kingdom'. But if the object of that worship is displaced, idolatry results. As we saw in the discussion about the nature of democracy, our longing for God can degenerate into authoritarianism if we claim that in this life we can experience the kingdom of God in its fullness. As O'Donovan writes:

> The doctrine that *we* set up political authority, as a device to secure our own essentially private, local and unpolitical purposes, has left the western democracies in a state of pervasive moral debilitation, which, from time to time,

inevitably throws up idolatrous and authoritarian reactions.[33]

When Jesus came to declare the coming of the kingdom of God, he came to perform miracles of power, to draw the vulnerable and oppressed into the kingdom community and to declare God's mercy, love and justice. He came to draw Israel into the fulfilment of their own history, and his kingship was rejected by them. He came to save the world, and in doing so changed the meaning of society and the purpose of its structures. The church now represents his kingdom. He came to judge the world, doing away with the old order. He came to restore creation, doing away with death and bringing a new creation. He rose from the dead and was exalted, thereby calling us into the new world. He is King of kings and Lord of lords, and not only Christians but all powers are subject to him. We are to submit to our rulers, but our primary allegiance is to Christ.

Rulers are to act as God would act, rewarding good and punishing evil. They are to allow Christ's work to continue in the world, through the church. One day their leadership will no longer be needed, because 'every eye shall see' Christ[34] and acknowledge that he is the source of all authority. Until then, the church will sometimes have to confront the state, being one of those voices ordained to remind it of its duty. The church is called to be the body of Christ and to represent to the world what God is like. In doing so, it will both celebrate and suffer. Because of who God is, we are called to remind the state of its obligation to govern by maintaining the freedom of people made in the image of God; to govern justly but with mercy, as God does; to preserve freedom of speech and to maintain those structures, such as family, law and tradition, that are essential if human community is to flourish.

As this chapter closes, how can we draw its strands together? An important theme is that we currently live in a world that has been compromised and is therefore provisional. The church is here to witness to the kingdom of God in all its aspects. In a world without God, things in many areas of life are not as they should be. There is individualism rather than community, rights without responsibilities, abuse of political authority, the excesses of market capitalism and the confusion of a post-ideological world regarding how power should be distributed. In this context, the church is called to be deeply involved in working out its own mission while waiting with longing for a new age to dawn. We are living in the light of a promise, and, whatever the spirit of the age, the job of the church is to convey that promise to the world through living out the message at the heart of its four voices of responsibility, celebration, prophecy and suffering.

The world in which we live is becoming increasingly enamoured of its own power. The technological society is not just about our ability to make things. It is changing the way we see the world. It challenges our longing for the world to come by rooting us in our ability to control our own future. Technology is changing what we believe about our world and therefore about ourselves. We find ourselves up against powers that are changing our vision of what it means to be human. These are the issues we shall explore next.

7
The impact of technological change

In a Soho restaurant the drinks waitress moves around the room. But in this case the waitress, speaking in dulcet tones, is a metre high stainless steel cube that chatters its way around on rubber wheels.

Technology transforms the world. Sometimes it does so in frivolous or seemingly trivial ways, but it is still powerful. It takes what we have learned about the world and applies it to changing that world, but it uses a restricted kind of knowledge: technical knowledge. All technical development omits facets of human behaviour and community, because technical knowledge cannot describe or analyse people or their communities in anything but the most rudimentary way.

Assessing technology

How do we begin to assess technology? There are eight issues we need to take into account before we can start to answer that question.

First, technology is not good or bad in itself, but it can be put to good or bad uses. Pessimistically to reject its claims to bring about a better world, or naïvely to accept them, is to refuse to think ethically about it. Nothing can be assumed about technology; it has to be assessed. Yet it is easy to be carried along by the pace of change. New technology can produce a sense of wonder and excitement that sometimes detracts from our willingness to step back and consider what is happening.

Second, technology always makes an impact on the world, by definition. Technology is applied thinking. It is not the same as an abstruse theorem which, however aesthetically pleasing, may have no immediate relevance to the real world. The very existence of technology depends on its ability to transform the world; otherwise it will have failed in its objectives. Its effects are never neutral.

Third, it has unintended consequences. This is partly because of our inability to peer into the future, but also partly because of technology's necessary reductionism, mentioned above. What is the effect of the internet on human relationships? The subject is still hotly debated.

Fourth, debate about technology tends to take place at its frontier, where its impact is most obvious. In a fast-changing society, it is possible to overlook the effects of powerful technologies that have been subsumed into the system too quickly. Drugs may be tested and released on to the market, and years later may be found to have dangerous side effects. These might have been discovered and dealt with, had not there been so much commercial pressure to get the product to market in the shortest possible time.

Fifth, technology cannot be uninvented. Once it is introduced, the only possibility of constraining it is by legislation or by issuing of codes of ethics that curb its uses.

Sixth, technology changes the human imagination. The invention of atomic, biological and chemical weapons means that every assessment of political tension between nations includes an assessment of the likelihood of their use. The invention of new technologies changes our view of our future, our world and ourselves.

Seventh, technology has a spiritual dimension. People discover and apply it with creative energies which are gifts from God. But since all of us are fallen, these energies can be distorted and used for evil purposes. Technology can become a force for good that can be celebrated, or it can align itself with those powers that have a destructive force.

Eighth, technology has widespread effects on employment and on local community life and thus changes the map of human need. For instance, the invention of the modem and the personal computer means that more people can work from home. Although this may be convenient for some, homeworking raises issues about the need for offices, the services that supply them (cleaners, restaurants, etc.) as well as the loneliness that can affect homeworkers. Inevitably, some gain from the changes while others lose. In the case of the medical profession, much of the work of diagnosis performed by doctors may disappear as self-diagnosis kits become more acceptable. Are the gains worth the losses? Sometimes we find out only with hindsight, as those knock-on effects take time to become evident. By the time we have reached a conclusion, the new map is in place, for good or ill.

The task of assessing technological change, therefore, turns out to be both essential and difficult. Sometimes we get it wrong. Over the last 200 years, we have been fortunate that, with some notable and disastrous exceptions, much technological development has served to increase the quality of human life. Recently, voices have been raised which claim that we have entered an entirely new situation in which we are at risk from the consequences of our own technological successes. If so, the task of assessment and the call to prophetic resistance will become an urgent vocation for the Christian church.

Technical and religious knowledge

In many parts of the Third World, little has changed for hundreds of years. Primitive tools increase the productivity of workers as they till the soil or harvest rice. But they do not influence the worldview of those who use them. They are extensions of the worker's body making her efforts more effective. A chisel remains a tool under the control of its user. Occasionally an invention changes the course of people's lives, as when the invention of the longbow changed the way battles were fought. Even so, medieval war was still fought within a given religious worldview.

The advent of Galileo, the telescope and scientific observation began to challenge the accepted religious paradigm, and battle was joined as a result. With the work of Kepler and Copernicus, the church's insistence that the Earth was at the centre of the universe, and therefore the place of theology in describing the universe, began to be questioned. This was for three reasons. First, although the first scientific observations were rudimentary, they could be repeatedly tested and shown to be correct: they were open to question, which theology was not. Secondly, technology was more powerful than theology in making the physical world both visible and understandable. Looking through a telescope or microscope could evoke a greater sense of wonder at creation than being in a church service could. The scientific analysis of nature should never have become an alternative to the theology of creation in this way, but should have remained a partner with it. Thirdly, theologians had overreached themselves by claiming that theology could explain more than it actually could. They had used theological knowledge to make technical statements about the universe which were not affirmed by the Scriptures.

As religious and technical knowledge appeared to become detached from each other, religion became more focused on individual faith. In many ways technology as revelation took the place of worship. The technological was seen to do more for people. As one writer has put it, 'instead of prayer there was now penicillin'.[1]

Moving away from wisdom[2]

This move from a public theological paradigm to a public technological paradigm is paralleled by three shifts in the kind of knowledge that technological societies facilitate, as sociologist Neil Postman points out. The first is the shift *from wisdom to knowledge*. Wisdom is not dependent on technology. It is based on human observation of the world and is primarily passed down through relationship. Of course, it contains knowledge, but of a significantly different kind. The theological paradigm claimed authority on the basis of its received wisdom, and disaster resulted when the gatekeepers of that worldview were seen to be wrong and its wisdom came into question. Wisdom, like freedom, depends on recognizing limits. Knowledge is different. It does not depend on wisdom. It can be learnt and passed on without leading to wisdom. It is possible to take in knowledge and then churn it out for exams or other tests without it affecting the way we see the world or live within it. The aim of the teacher is to bring wisdom and knowledge together in the pupil's imagination, but in a society that moves fast there is often no time for that. In contemporary Britain, results have come to dominate reflection.

If the first move is from wisdom to knowledge, the second is *from knowledge to information*. Just as wisdom is not dependent on technology, information is not necessarily dependent on humanity. There is no reason why information should have anything to do with human interests or human purposes. We are currently in an information glut. Does that information work for humanity, or against it? The exploitation of information as a traded commodity may, as with all commodities, have good and/or bad consequences. Access to information, for instance through the internet, is currently exciting us all. We can see a 'revolution of possibilities' in it. But the way we deal with that information will decide whether it has added to the sum total of our knowledge as a human community. Many children may have access to a computer encyclopedia and can do their homework by looking it up. Quite apart from the fact that children are tending to produce all the same answers because they use the same software, can they be said to have acquired knowledge when all they have done is copy out information, or (worse) print it out?

The third shift completes the picture: the shift *from information to data*. Data is information in machine-stored form. Even if we analyse it, for instance in the form of economic statistics, it is still data in machine-stored form. A great deal of the information in the world is in the form of data readable only by machines. A lot of knowledge about me is stored in the form of data.

Within a fast-changing technological society, then, there is a shift from wisdom to knowledge to information to data. It is a shift from the qualitative to the quantitative, and produces a bias towards technological change and away from the maintenance of tradition. Once this cycle is started, it is difficult to stop, as it involves a self-reinforcing belief that the technological future is always better than the traditional past. This may be true of the technological *product*, which may go from one improvement to another, but is it true of the technological *society*? Before we can discuss this in detail, we must look at the rise of technology and its impact on society.

In the period up to the twentieth century, British and American invention produced a burst of innovation. Technology increased its momentum as railways, telephones, moving pictures and medical advances made an impact. The world was opened up, and people whose relationships had been restricted to the immediate vicinity began to travel and discover places and cultures they had never known before. The results were spectacular. Mobility, communication and hygiene were all improved. At this time, much of the knowledge on which technological developments were based served human purposes and meaning. These developments increased a sense of community and individuality. They enabled people to keep in touch with family. Education became more widely available. Medicine enabled people to live healthier lives. Knowledge, understanding and human purposes seemed to go hand in hand.

In his book *Technopoly*, Neil Postman divides the development of technology into three ages. In the first age, tools are used and controlled by people. In the second, which he calls 'technocracy', technology serves human purposes, but the balance between the person and the technology is beginning to change. In the textile mills, for instance, machines did the weaving, so people became machine-minders rather than being creative themselves. Were men and women using the machine or were they serving the machine? The balance was changing. In the third age, called a 'technopoly', technology cuts its ties with human meaning and purposes and develops autonomy. This is the age which, Postman suggests, we are entering at the moment.

As the power of technology increased, then, the balance of power was shifting between human beings and machines. People increasingly became machine-minders. It was true that human creativity was transferred into designing and making the machines, even if the craft skills had been displaced. It was also true that these industrial processes were more efficient and were the source of unrivalled wealth creation. Technology, like the economic markets that developed around it, produced wealth, but distributed it unequally. Key ethical issues were raised which are still on the agenda of both church and society.

Technology can bring extraordinary benefit to people as the very best of human gifts and callings are put to good use. But it can also displace human abilities, erode human dignity, destroy human community, lead to idolatry and misdirect human creativity. When it does so, the church must speak out on behalf of those who are affected. Many people in the West are still working in 'sweatshops' for less than the minimum wage, with poor conditions and long hours – to say nothing of the sweatshops of the East.

Progress, efficiency and convenience

It is not easy to recognize the need for a prophetic vision, because technological development, as with economic worldviews generally, is sold to us in terms of progress and efficiency. It is true that we have progressed technologically, even though we may not have progressed morally. But we have tended to ally technological progress with moral progress. The movement away from morality based on divine revelation has meant that some moral claims have become self-referencing. Claims to progress, efficiency and convenience are good examples of this.

As with all self-referencing points in modernity, such claims serve no higher moral purpose, and cannot do so, by definition. That would require a revealed given. When these lower-order moral claims became dominant, technology began to cut itself adrift from human purposes, and technological autonomy became possible. In Postman's terms, it became possible that western culture would move from technocracy to technopoly.

It is difficult to argue against progress. The same is true of efficiency. How can we defend inefficiency as a good thing? How can we argue against convenience? These are the arguments used to sell us new technology. Their effectiveness depends on the equation of three values: technological progress equals human progress equals moral progress. It is important to challenge this. We can argue that technical developments are not morally acceptable, do not promote human purposes or may be detrimental to human life itself. The moral debate about new technology is constantly skewed by the fact that we know what the new technology can do, and we think that just because it is new it is an improvement. But since we cannot see into the future, we do not know what its negative consequences might be. Debate about these is more speculative, and seems less substantial then the positive contribution the new technology will make.

Technology can also over-extend itself by straying into areas in which it has no rights or authority. As already noted, is based on technical knowledge. It filters out other kinds of knowledge in order to be precise. Take as an example a recent report which claimed that people who pray are less anxious and depressed than those who do not. This conclusion, drawn from psychological testing, seems to have authority because expert opinion is backed up by technical knowledge. In this case Christians are smug. The report supports our own views. But this joyful news is a Trojan horse. The technical paradigm has overreached itself in purporting to say something about the effectiveness of prayer. How do we know they were praying? Perhaps it was a measure of people who lied about praying. Prayer cannot be measured – only the claim to be praying. If experts who are not committed to a Christian paradigm begin to assess Christianity scientifically, the result will be not only reductionist but also expressed in technical rather than theological language. Sin will become 'deviance' and worship will become 'transference'. Here again we see the clash between technical knowledge and theological knowledge, although this time the assault is subtler.

To summarize, we have developed from wisdom to knowledge, and all cultures everywhere have a mix of both. Knowledge that is increasingly technical has dominated the last hundred years. We ask not *why* we do things, but *how* we do them. We are excited and awed by the fact that we *can* do them at all. But now knowledge seems to be cut adrift from human purposes. We are also coming up against the unintended consequences of human action,[3] such as pollution and other environmental problems.[4] Our excessive awe of building technologies has obliterated a sense of human community for many. We have replaced purpose by momentum. Instead of living with a self-referencing technology which is increasingly out of control, we need to find an alternative platform. Otherwise we shall simply attempt to solve our problems by generating even more technology.

In 1979, Jean-François Lyotard raised the issue of the nature of knowledge in a technological society and saw the 'information-processing machine' as changing the way we learn. He saw learning as being transformed into 'quantities of information'. He went as far as to say that knowledge incapable of translation into computer language will be discarded.

The old principle that the acquisition of knowledge is

indissociable from the training (*Bildung*) of minds, or even of individuals, is becoming obsolete and will become ever more so. The relationship of the suppliers and users of knowledge to the knowledge they supply and use is now tending, and will increasingly tend, to assume the form already taken by the relationship of commodity producers and consumers to the commodities they produce and consume – that is, the form of value. Knowledge is and will be produced in order to be sold, it is and will be consumed in order to be valorised in a new production: in both cases, the goal is exchange. Knowledge ceases to be an end in itself, it loses its 'use-value'.[5]

What is the difference between information increasingly expressed as data, and human knowledge? We have already observed that there is no reason for information to have any link to human purposes. Already, information is a fiercely traded commodity to which the West owes much of its economic life. But knowledge should not be a commodity, and should have a human context. Postman examines the way in which, over time, we have created human institutions in which knowledge becomes significant, such as education, the judiciary, science and government. We have ways of pursuing knowledge so that it adds not only to some aspect of human understanding, but also to knowledge already received and categorized according to subject matter. As Neil Postman points out, the existence of a curriculum within education represents a decision by the community that every young person should be taught certain essential elements of knowledge. Knowledge links humanity and the world we live in. If knowledge becomes divorced from understanding, we become impoverished, even though as a culture we own vast intellectual resources.

As philosopher Mary Midgley points out, we all need a mental map of the priority systems by which we judge between various forms of knowledge. This power of selection is a part of wisdom:

> A remarkable attempt has been made in [the twentieth] century to withdraw the notion of knowledge from this province of thought, indeed to cut it off radically from the

rest of life. When knowledge is secluded in this way and equated with information, understanding is pushed into the background and the notion of wisdom is quite forgotten.[6]

Who benefits if our desire for knowledge as human beings ends up by being dominated by the scientific-technological paradigm? Midgley asks whether one of the 'great prizes of human endeavour', the pursuit of knowledge, will be handed over to machines and will belong to them rather than to us. Is this, she asks, the final result of the insatiable desire for knowledge that is one of the most exalted characteristics of our species?

> There are, of course, people today who apparently quite like this idea, and call on us to be well satisfied if our machines do important things for us better than we do. But just which important things? The function before us now – that of characteristically human enjoyment, of fulfilment, of receiving the highest gratifications of which humanity is capable – does not seem to be one which it would make sense to hand over to others and even have performed for one. 'Live? Our servants can do that for us,' said Whistler. But people only say that sort of thing about aspects of living which they want to reject entirely.[7]

As she points out, knowing and understanding are part of our being; they are not personal possessions. This is crucial if we are to understand the role the church must play in an information society. Reflection on these changes must lead us constantly to compare those attitudes to knowledge that are based on *having* with those that express *being*. Knowledge as possession is a hallmark of information societies. Knowledge as understanding is a hallmark of relational communities. Certainly the Bible is committed to wisdom as an important, and essentially relational, way of teaching us how to live. That commitment does not change just because the culture in which we are trying to live as Christians is postmodern.

Part of our problem is that information overload is occurring just when some of the traditional elements of our culture, which have limited and therefore focused knowledge, are under strain. In a postmodern age the definition of knowledge breaks down. Postman comments that within mainstream education we teach astronomy but not astrology, religion but not magic. As a community, we have made decisions not only about priorities but also about what constitutes knowledge as opposed to superstition. When knowledge drifts free from any sense of objective truth, distinctions between these subjects begin to disappear. Courses appear on subjects such as witchcraft and crystal healing, which, though popular, are at odds with the western tradition's most basic understanding of what constitutes knowledge. All knowledge exists in context, and the seismic shift occurring in our society is leading to a collapse in traditional structures of knowledge.

In a postmodern technopoly, where information of all sorts is being thrown at us, the moral commitments that allowed us to filter out good information from bad have fragmented. Postman quotes the family as one institution which traditionally instils values in children, protects them from inappropriate influences, and allows them access to certain words and ideas only when they are mature enough to cope with them. From this perspective, the family is a manager of information. This function depends on knowing what the family is for. There is a prior moral vision central to the existence of the family which enables it to be what Christopher Lasch has called 'a haven in a heartless world'.[8] But such is the torrent of information now aimed at children that it is now impossible to monitor what they are being exposed to. The volume of the information is due to its commercialization.

The concept of educational institutions and the family as instruments for controlling information so as to build both community and individuality is important in our consideration of contemporary culture. In our liberal societies, the dominant idea of freedom is that anybody should have access to whatever they want. The idea that family life has been given to us by God as the context in which children gradually discover what it means to be free under the guidance of loving parents is seen as not only passé but a threat to children's rights. The volume of information, especially in the media and on the internet, together with the weakening of family authority, makes the line of least resistance seem attractive. Taking it can include lowering the age at which children watch inappropriate material. All this can happen when families find it difficult to monitor what their children are watching. When children have televisions and internet access in their bedrooms, it should come as no surprise that they watch material that is too adult for them. Liberal democracy, as we are experiencing it at present, is defenceless against the rapid pace of technological change because it lacks those prior moral commitments that would enable it to shape information into creative knowledge.

As Postman points out, the Bible is another instrument for filtering out information so that knowledge becomes consistent with a given worldview. He helpfully links the issue of religiously motivated information control to the rise of technology:

> The Bible gives manifold instructions on what one must do and must not do, as well as guidance on what language to avoid (on pain of committing blasphemy), what ideas to avoid (on pain of committing heresy), what symbols to avoid (on pain of committing idolatry). Necessarily, but perhaps unfortunately, the Bible also explained how the world came into being in such literal detail that it could not accommodate new information produced by the telescope and subsequent technologies. The trials of Galileo and, three hundred years later, of Scopes were therefore about the admissibility of certain kinds of information. Both Cardinal Bellarmine and William Jennings Bryan were fighting to maintain the authority of the Bible to control information about the profane world as well as the sacred. In their defeat more was lost than the Bible's claim to explain the origins and structure of nature. The Bible's authority in defining and categorising moral behaviour was also weakened.[9]

Rejecting the authority of the Bible and the relevance of Christianity leaves us even more awash with information, some of which is destructive, without the moral commitments to filter out the good from the bad and the useful from the trash.

Accountability

As a culture, we are also struggling with issues of accountability. These can be focused around three points: the relationship between science and technology, the power of the multinationals and the driven nature of technology.

First, the distinction between science and technology is breaking down. Previously, scientists claimed that they were doing pure research and that their work (the pursuit of knowledge for its own sake) was value-free – a view that has been disputed since the work of Thomas Kuhn and Michael Polyani. Scientists are no longer funded by government grants as much as they once were. Such grants went some way to guaranteeing their independence. But many research projects are now funded by industry. Without impugning the integrity of the individuals concerned, they are inevitably under pressure to produce results that will benefit those who fund them. Corporations want a return on their investment. This has particularly worrying consequences when committees that decide whether to license contentious technologies are increasingly staffed by scientists who may have vested interests in the decisions made. Added to this is the fact that the general public is now more suspicious of scientists. Problems such as BSE in the UK agricultural industry have drawn attention to the limits of science and the fallibility of scientists. As a result, accountability has become more complex, embracing both the developer of the application and the deviser of the idea behind it.

Secondly, there is considerable concern about the size of multinational corporations and their dominance in world markets. They are the primary carriers of globalization, in that they are not constrained by frontiers. They pay scant attention to differences in cultures, except in so far as marketing demands it. It is a familiar cliché that the economies of many multinationals are bigger than those of some nation states, and their ability to affect global economic life is considerable. There have been several attempts to regulate their behaviour by voluntary codes of ethics, but the ability of multinationals to move money and resources around the world makes it difficult to track their behaviour. The scale of the multinationals leads many people to be fatalistic about the possibility of controlling them, where that would be appropriate.

Yet four constraints on their power do exist. (1) All large corporations, which trade on their reputation in free markets, are vulnerable to investigative journalism and consumer campaigns. (2) Those who do not wish to support multinationals by buying their products turn to alternative outlets that sell 'ethical' products. An example is the fair-trade organization Traidcraft in the UK which imports goods from the Third World, paying indigenous workers and producers fair wages and prices. (3) In an age of rapid technological change there is an unprecedented opportunity for single entrepreneurs to compete with multinationals. The ferment of change in Silicon Valley, California, is not all due to the giants such as Microsoft. Many of the most exciting developments started when one person or a small group of people had an idea. Such innovation can undermine the work of multinationals, which may be slow to respond to it. (4) It is possible for governments to bring corporations to heel where there is a strong tradition of commercial law. The US government recently won a case against Microsoft, which was accused of operating a software monopoly. It is true that Third World countries do not have the resources to fight such battles. Nevertheless, there are Third World corporations big enough to take over western companies, and recent takeovers by companies in India and South Korea show that globalization will eventually have an impact in all directions.

Thirdly, a frequent outcome of the powerful marriage of technology and commercialism is fatalism. 'If we don't do it, someone else will.' In commercial terms, to neglect this argument is to risk going under. This is what determines the 'driven' nature of technology. To be at the frontier of technology is to be part of a race. The excitement is matched only by the stress participation generates. Here is one of the key dangers of modern technology: the decision to go ahead is not voluntary, but is forced by the possibility that a competitor might get there first. A prior commitment to commercial realities makes the response inevitable. The technology comes first, and the ethics second. Increased specialization of employment within technology means that employees feel trapped on a treadmill that is increasing in speed. Those who are not finding the pace exhilarating feel powerless. In Silicon Valley, the whiz-kids

The impact of technological change

are very young. For a time at least, they thrive on the adrenaline rush that keeps them at their computers for sixty hours a week or more.

Indeed, some argue that the pace is accelerating, and that our attitude to time is changing as a result. In a recent book on the acceleration of change,[10] James Gleick argues that we are increasingly frustrated by the time things take. How many of us have lost patience with lift doors that seem slow to close, and jabbed the 'close door' button even though we knew it would have no further effect? Computer rage has joined road rage as people try to fill their day with too many tasks and then vent their frustration on their technology or on the people around them. We cannot waste time; to do so would contravene the law of efficiency. If we can go faster we must; to question this is unthinkable. Yet, like the Red Queen in *Through the Looking-Glass*, as we go faster nothing much seems to change. Here the Judeo-Christian concept of Sabbath is prophetic, as is an insistence on the primacy of relationships, especially the time given to family life. Yet we all suspect one another of going the same way, and family meals even in Christian households, are reduced to Sunday lunch if we are lucky.

We are adapting to the pace of technology, rather than resisting it in the name of an alternative vision for human life. As I have already indicated, such an adaptation diminishes us as human beings. The fact that we do not change indicates that we are driven by the fear that, if we do slow down, we shall be overtaken by those who are quite willing to go for the ride. Such technologies do not express or extend creativity, but have become distorted, and are perhaps even tyrannical in their impact on human life. Notice that the problem is as much with the building or development of the technology as with the impact of the finished product on human society.

The World Wide Web

When Tim Berners-Lee designed the World Wide Web as an application to be used at CERN, the European particle-physics laboratory in Geneva, he could not have guessed at the impact it would have on the world via the internet.

In his autobiographical account of the development of the Web,

Berners-Lee tells of how the idea started from a desire to give members of the scientific community the ability to share information despite the fact that they were using different hardware and codes. He did not want computers to be connected to a central server that would control access, but envisaged an open space in which anybody could access any information on a computer anywhere. Since few people were interested in his work, at least in the early stages, his determination to achieve his dream is remarkable.

In 1980 he took a brief consulting job at CERN, and it was here that he wrote his first Web-like program. But it was not until Christmas Day 1990 that his World Wide Web browser/editor was up and running and communicating with the internet, linking not only files but also newsgroups and articles. Berners-Lee began to measure the number of people accessing the computer at CERN on the World Wide Web. The project was rapidly gaining momentum. The rate was doubling every three or four months, and growing by a factor of ten every year. In the summer of 1991 it counted 100 hits a day, rising to 1,000 in the summer of 1992 and 10,000 in the summer of 1993.

Berners-Lee did not start his own company, although he could have become rich if he had. He occasionally talked about having a personal ethic that rejected the measurement of a person's worth by the amount of money he or she possessed. His vision for the Web was not what it could do for him, but what it could do for others. Interestingly, he always focused on people, acknowledging that although one could communicate with people by email, it was exciting to meet together, face to face. He became director of a consortium of institutions that used the Web, which created standards and recommendations that were then distributed to the industry for their use (WC3). However, this was not an attempt to control:

> Whether inspired by free-market desires or humanistic ideals, we all felt that control was the wrong perspective. I made it clear that I had designed the Web so that there should be no centralised place where someone would have to 'register' a new server, or get approval of its contents. Anybody could build a server and put anything on it. Philosophically, if the

Web was to be a universal resource, it had to be able to grow in an unlimited way. Technically, if there was a centralised point of control, it would rapidly become a bottleneck that restricted the Web's growth, and the Web would never scale up. Its 'being out of control' was very important.[11]

In these early stages of the Web, the ideals Berners-Lee had for it predominated. This changed when the Web became more commercial and profits began to be made. Technology stocks changed hands for enormous sums of money, and suddenly the internet, accessed by the Web, became the place to make money. Nevertheless, he still saw the Web as something that would bring great good to the world. He describes a meeting of the G7 nations, held in February 1995 in Brussels, where the role of rapidly advancing technology was on the agenda.

> ... the keynote speaker was Thabo Mbeki, then deputy president of South Africa. Mbeki delivered a profound speech on how people should seize the new technology to empower themselves, to keep themselves informed about the truth of their own economic, political and cultural circumstances; and to give themselves a voice that all the world could hear. I could not have written a better mission statement for the World Wide Web.[12]

It was IBM that first broached the subject of pornography on the Web at the consortium. There was concern that children might have access to it. The response from other members of the consortium, however, was to protest that the Web was an example of free speech. Nevertheless, the US Congress passed the Communications Decency Act which was challenged in the courts by civil-rights groups and thrown out. The industry's response was to devise a series of programs that would filter out any objectionable material. They could be readily installed by parents, without payment. This had the merit of protecting children, but did nothing to stem the burgeoning adult porn market. The word most frequently searched for on the net was 'sex'. Freedom of speech, combined with the privacy of access in the home meant that every aspect of human life was represented on the Web, from the beauty of the world's art galleries to hard-core child pornography. The empowerment of the disenfranchised of the world went hand in hand with their continued exploitation. It was impossible to separate the good from the bad or the useful from the trash.

Does the increase in information, such as we now have access to on the Web, lead to an increase in wisdom? I think we can definitely respond in the negative. Here is a prime example of the move from knowledge to information. It appears that much of this information does not serve human purposes. Berners-Lee saw that the Web had to be 'out of control' if it was to work. But it has become a major source of an information glut, which is also out of control. We now have to find ways of restoring that control.

The internet highlights the familiar tension between democratic freedoms and civil order. The amount of hard-core pornography on the Web is astonishing. The kinds of porn available are so violent and degrading that many feel we must do something, but the debate is in its early stages and protests about censorship are everywhere. Organizations such as Childnet International are being set up to promote good practice on the Web and also to campaign against child pornography. Another problem is the abuse of privacy. Several Web experts have said that every time you use email, you must assume that someone is monitoring you. Other issues raised by use of the Web concern the possibility of policing corrupt material internationally, the effectiveness of voluntary codes of conduct,[13] the impact of the internet on personal relationships, and the possibility of using the Web in Third World contexts for education and commercial purposes.

There are a lot of applications of new technology in the Third World. We saw earlier that globalization can be a disruptive force in the world, but it can also facilitate some very positive changes. New technology, like money, is unevenly distributed both throughout the world and within countries, causing new inequalities. But it is also providing opportunities for developing societies to open up a new economic sector which depends primarily on intellectual resources. Access to this requires an increased commitment to provide education throughout the world, and in many countries few have access even to primary education. Nevertheless, many countries are benefiting from the digital revolution. We often stereotype this situation by saying that the North has new technology while the South does not, which is mostly true. There are more computers in the United States than in the rest of the world combined, and more telephones in Tokyo than in the whole of Africa. Two billion people in the world have never made a phone call. Yet things are changing. Bangalore has become a city of innovation, with 300 high-tech companies. India's software exports alone exceeded $4bn in 2000 (about 9% of its total exports). Its software industry is set to increase to $85bn by 2008. Costa Rica's economic growth surged to 8.3% in 1999 – the highest in Latin America, fuelled by exports from the microchip industry, which now accounts for 38% of all its exports.

Mauritius uses the internet to position its textile industry globally. Tiny operations anywhere can now trade products on-line, like the crafts-based co-operative in Peru that linked up with a broker in New York and increased its net income threefold as a result. Mali uses the Net for more effective administration, and other countries for telemedicine or banking. Telecentres have been established in places as remote from the centres of commerce as Kazakhstan. The United Nations has centres in Mongolia's Gobi Desert where local people can log on and be trained in the use of computers. Third World students are also benefiting from UN investment into computer skills. Several organizations have started up with the aim of bringing the Net to the Third World. Netaid.org aims to link people in the Northern Hemisphere to people in the South, enabling the latter to offer their expertise as 'virtual volunteers'. Despite these efforts, the lack of access to the Net, and its high cost, may well lead to frustrations in the short term.

This should not discourage us, so that we opt out of the struggle. It just means that access to new technology must be factored into the equation both in opening up new opportunities and in identifying new forms of poverty. Provision of information technology to those who want access to markets can revolutionize their businesses, and there are many stories of business people in the Third World who have benefited as a result. Conversely, it can exacerbate the poverty within a culture, as those with access to the global economy through the internet draw away from those without.

Access to the internet means access to globalization and the prospect of making money through markets. Yet increased income is not its only effect on our lives. New technology is also changing the way we communicate with one another. Email is an efficient way of communicating, and it fits in with the time pressures we are under. There is no doubt that email enables us to contact people with an immediacy that 'snail mail' could never dream of. Yet sentences on a screen are not the same as face-to-face meetings. We grow up in small communities where intimacy is important to us. Although we can make electronic connections with many people, they have a tendency to spread us too thinly and can contribute to the problem of the 'saturated self' we have already discussed. An email world is a superficial world. It will not solve the problems of the Prozac Nation. To the extent that technology deceives us into thinking that we have many good relationships, it does us harm rather than good. One good friend is worth a million friendly emails.

Technological change is driving our society at such a pace that it makes ever-increasing demands on us. Consequently, we are becoming increasingly stressed as a community, but feel powerless to resist. Ironically, at the same time, we are excited about the possibilities that technology is opening up, and are genuinely delighted at the benefits these will create for our children and grandchildren. We can only hope that the impact of each new technology is benevolent. Even if we were clear about our ethical commitments as a culture, they would lag behind the development of the technology. All the while this is happening, we are awash in a flood of information that we cannot control. The institutions set up to prioritize this information, such as education, family and religion, have all become so battered in postmodern culture that they now have little authority with which to exercise that role. The inventor of the World Wide Web sees its as being 'out of control' as a virtue. Contemporary attitudes to rights means that controlling even the worst excesses of the Web is problematic. In an age of globalization, issues of accountability become crucial as nations have to co-operate across frontiers to be effective.

Wisdom is at a discount in the world, but sharing vast amounts of information cannot produce it. Something that is not produced wisely cannot add to wisdom. It can only increase our awareness of our need for it, or of the sterility of a culture without it. Our problem is that our excitement at the ingenuity of our technology has blinded our eyes to our lack of wisdom. The dualism behind the world of technology and the world of the human, the impersonal and the personal, is finally proving too much for us, and some are beginning to ask what our superb technology is *for*. How is it possible for us to be clever enough to design something as powerful as the internet, only to find it distributing pornography at a time when we are so morally weak that we no longer know how to speak in terms of right and wrong?

The technological society is one that Christians should celebrate warily. It is what technology is *for* that counts. We need to remain close to God so that we can hear his voice despite all the excitement going on around us. As the Bible says, 'The fear of the LORD is the beginning of wisdom.'[14]

8
The Spirit working in us

One of the questions raised in the last chapter was, 'Whose purpose does technology serve?' This is a question not primarily about vested interests, but about whether technology furthers God's purposes for the world or not. Indeed, in each of the topics we have been considering, this is the main issue at stake. Are we using those gifts that God has given us in a way that is itself godly? Does our presence as Christians in the community speak of the kingdom of God? Are we people who, being secure in God, have something to offer a fractured community? We stay with the subject of technology as we look at its use in relation to God's purposes.

Use and abuse

At the outset of this book we saw that God is committed to culture, evidenced by the fact that he creates us as bodily beings and embeds us in culture. God is thereby committed to technology, because it reflects both his and our creativity. It enables us to carry out our mandate to be trustees of the world. Within the sphere of technology the four marks of the church's involvement with the world are still important. Our responsibility to the world, celebration of the world, prophecy to the world and suffering with the world are all elements of life that technology can reflect and affect. It is easier to listen to a piece of music and celebrate it than to look at the design of a lorry and do the same. Yet the technical designer is using God-given talents as much as the musician. One crafts sound, the other metal and rubber.

The Spirit working in us 155

Throughout human history, gifted craftspeople have not only been used to build the housing, hospitals, transport, schools and factories that are necessary in our life as a community; they have also used their gifts to express worship. Bezalel was appointed by God to construct the tabernacle, its furniture, the altar and the Ark of the Covenant. He was helped by Oholiab. These two, along with the many craftsmen taught by them, are not well known in Scripture, but they do not need to be. It was their work that was important.

> See I have chosen Bezalel son of Uri, the son of Hur, of the tribe of Judah, and I have filled him with the Spirit of God, with skill, ability and knowledge in all kinds of crafts – to make artistic designs for work in gold, silver and bronze, and to engage in all kinds of craftsmanship.[1]

This undertaking was something in which the whole community became involved. Those who had any of the necessary raw materials brought them as a sacrifice, and they were then incorporated into the work. It was not just that the finished work was to represent God's covenant with his people; the manner of its making was also covenantal. The tabernacle was the outcome of the work both of God and of the community. Here was a place where not only priests but also craftsmen, filled with the Holy Spirit, brought people near to God.

In an age of planned obsolescence, we are still in awe of our ancient cathedrals. They speak of an era that had different priorities. There too, craftspeople used their skill to bring glory to God. To walk into a cathedral is a humbling experience. People who wanted the finished work to bring glory to God imagined each aspect of the construction. Craftspeople then built it and embellished it over many decades, and we are led to worship because of it. Vision, construction and response are components of every technology, and here they are dedicated to God.

There is, then, both continuity and discontinuity between the craftsmen who built the tabernacle and the technologist who develops a new vacuum cleaner. Both use 'skill, ability and knowledge' given to them by God. They may even have prayed identical prayers, such as 'Lord, enable me to use my gifts for you today.' But

Bezalel and Oholiab, filled with the Holy Spirit, used their God-given skills in devotion to a holy cause, the result of which was the creation of a place where God could meet with his people.

Sadly, the Bible contains potent examples of the opposite use of human skill. The story of the tower of Babel focuses on a group of people who conspired to defeat God's purposes for the world. The means by which they chose to do this was technological.

> They said to each other, 'Come, let's make bricks and bake them thoroughly.' They used brick instead of stone, and bitumen for water. Then they said, 'Come, let us build ourselves a city, with a tower that reaches to the heavens, so that we might make a name for ourselves and not be scattered over the face of the whole earth.'[2]

In this case, people wanted to use technology to make a statement about themselves. They had found a place to settle and wanted to build a city. Two things stand out about their plans. First, they developed an immensely capable building technology. Their use of hard-baked bricks and bitumen enabled them to envisage a tower that could reach into the heavens. In other words, having used their 'skill, knowledge and ability' to develop a powerful technology, they then put it to evil use.

The tower represents their desire to 'make a name' for themselves. Their cleverness had given birth to arrogance. Having been made by God was no longer sufficient. They could take affairs into their own hands. As much in mercy as in judgment, God scattered them and confused their language.

Babel is an example of 'corporate evil' in that no one person is named as the perpetrator of the act. Whereas, in the making of the tabernacle, people are named by God, here there is an anonymous conspiracy against God. Presumably, people would have 'passed the buck' if questions had been asked. In both cases, the builders used their God-given gifts of 'skill, ability and knowledge'. But the purposes to which they put them could not have been further apart. The former reflected the glory of God; the latter invoked the judgment of God. In both cases, the use of technology is at the heart of the story.

Prayer in a technological society

Running throughout the Bible, and indeed throughout Christian history, is a recognition that prayer is a vital part of God-centred transformation of culture. But, in a technological society, how can people still believe that prayer can be a source of change? Prayer challenges the mindset of modernity. By praying, we learn to submit to the will of God. But we also believe that the world changes because of prayer. The apostle James urges us:

> ... confess your sins to each other and pray for each other so that you may be healed. The prayer of a righteous man is powerful and effective.
>
> Elijah was a man just like us. He prayed earnestly that it would not rain, and it did not rain on the land for three and a half years. Again he prayed, and the heavens gave rain, and the earth produced its crops.[3]

In the story of Elijah, righteous prayer and divine power work together. But in a technological society it is easy to look down on the foolishness of prayer from the dizzy heights of technology's accomplishments. This can in turn put pressure on Christians to portray prayer as a matter of cause and effect, like technology. We begin to see prayer as a another way of problem-solving. We become fixated on the ability of prayer to cause extraordinary and demonstrable effects. For most of us, however, prayer is conversation with God, and it is this conversation that enables us to see the extraordinary in the ordinary. In other words, prayer contributes to the development of a theology of everyday life. If we focus only on the extraordinary, we may risk becoming disillusioned, especially if we apply a model of prayer as problem-solving in the realm of healing. God does answer specific prayers. But the fact is that, from our myopic understanding of God's purposes, answers to prayer do look erratic when compared to the consistency of technological outcomes. We realize that as technology grows more powerful, the need for prayer seems to diminish. But we are not satisfied with prayer as an encounter with the mystery of God.

Instead of letting Elijah's prayer teach us about God's ways, we use his example as a rationale for viewing prayer as a way of producing results. Rather than being a conversation with God, it becomes part of the culture of efficiency. One of the most extreme illustrations of this was the recent attempt to show that, of two groups of ill people, the group that is prayed for will show a higher recovery rate than the control group. This is then attributed to the power of prayer. Whatever the results of such experiments, their very existence points to the pressure of the culture of efficiency in which we now live.

This pressure to demonstrate cause and effect in a technological society also highlights an extraordinary similarity between technology and magic. There is a strong link between cause and effect in magic. The incantations, astrological charts or crystals are there to produce or foresee an effect. Although the word 'faith' is sometimes mentioned, this is not faith as the Bible knows it. For Christians faith means following an invisible Christ because he is our Lord, whether or not we have specific signs or experiences of his presence. This is one of the problems people have with the Christian faith in a technological society. On the one hand, there is the great spiritual vision of God revealed in Christ, the work of salvation and the gift of grace. On the other, there is the common grace that we all receive because we are made in the image of God, though fallen. But there is a middle ground that Christianity does not seem to cover, resulting in frustration. People ask: 'Why did my son die in that car crash?' 'How can I know that I am marrying the right person?' As I write, I am myself in agony over a close friend who has just died in tragic circumstances. Why, God? Why?

These are among people's deepest questions, but there are no specific answers. This fact is difficult to cope with in an age of technology, which gives us the ability to be so precise in many aspects of life. We expect answers to these questions too. Folk magic (and even the questionnaires in popular magazines about how to find the perfect partner) tells us that such answers are available. The rise of the New Age in our society fills this gap. It is a protest against traditional religion in more ways than one. If we become frustrated with the absence of answers to such questions, the fascination with magic will continue – hence the growth of New Age philosophies in a scientific age. The two trends are not in opposition to each other, but are both drawing on human desire to be in control, whether through science or through incantation.

The religion of popular culture

Most Christians live in the world of popular theology, not of academic theology. In popular theology, biblical doctrine becomes fused with elements of popular culture to form diverse expressions of the Christian faith. It is easy for these to be despised as a lower form of theological life, without asking what popular religion has to teach us about how the Christian life should be lived. Such theology is portrayed everywhere in the festivals of the evangelical churches, such as (in Britain) Spring Harvest, New Wine or Greenbelt, and in the magazines and books attached to the sub-cultures they represent. Lay people need teaching in all aspects of theology in order to understand their faith more deeply and to learn more about God's purposes for their lives. Within these contexts there is a lot of life, commitment and wisdom from which we can learn.

This is not to say that we do not sometimes get it wrong and find ourselves in partnership with cultural forces that compromise the Christian faith. This chapter has already mentioned the tyranny of results in the context of prayer, for instance. It is also possible to get too enmeshed in the language and practice of the therapeutic society. If we succumb to these without reflection, we distort the faith. But this is not the same as looking down on popular expressions of faith and despising them because they are not to one's own taste. Richard Holloway, then Bishop of Edinburgh, once said that evangelical culture had tended towards 'fast food rather than haute cuisine'. But he admitted that the evangelical approach could be useful when it came to mission. 'More people go to discos than to high opera, and one of the courageous things about evangelicals is their ability to embrace bad taste for the sake of the gospel' (!).[4]

Theologian Richard Mouw advises us to approach popular culture with a 'hermeneutic of charity' rather than a 'hermeneutic of suspicion'. In other words, when people express their faith in unconventional ways (such as the young Christian executive who said he thought of God as the ultimate CEO), we should be willing to accept these unless they prove unhelpful.

> ... I hold to a 'transformationalist' view of Christ and culture. We cannot accept sinful culture as it is. But neither can we simply reject it as altogether evil. Cultural formation is part of the good creation. Contemporary culture, including contemporary popular culture, is a distorted version of something God meant to be good. So we must 'un-distort' it. We must look at such things as the current fascination with therapeutic techniques and managerial methods and ask how they might be transformed into instruments of obedience to the will of God. And we must be careful that, in opposing popular culture, we are not doing so out of an uncritical commitment to a 'high' culture that is itself in need of Christian transformation. It may be that the trends in popular culture, whatever their own distortions, are legitimate reactions against the kind of distortions to which intellectuals are especially prone.[5]

Pronouncements from on high are all very well, but they are next to useless if they do not take root in the lives of ordinary believers. We live our lives in the concrete and the complex. Many Christians will openly say that a sermon by a high flyer went right over their heads. One of the characteristics that make such preachers poor communicators is that they do not take the time to speak *into* the context in which their hearers find themselves. For instance, many men and women who are in full-time employment find sermons irrelevant because they do not address the world of work. These people probably see more of their colleagues than of their families. They face their greatest ethical dilemmas at work, as well as their greatest opportunities to live as Christians.

Lay people have a great deal of wisdom about how to apply the Christian faith in the world. This fact means that we must examine popular culture not only to reach out to it but also to gain theological insights from it. This is what this book has attempted to do. We have looked at some of the key themes that confront us in contemporary society, and have tried, explicitly or implicitly, to reflect on them. But even this task has been placed in an intellectual framework. It is important to acknowledge that wisdom comes in many different forms and may be distinct from formal knowledge.

As Richard Mouw comments, since only God's grace can save us, educated people are no more able to find God than the uneducated, and theologians have no better access to God than farmers or waitresses.[6] This does not mean that lay people can be left to their own theological devices. They need help from academic theologians and from wise pastors and teachers. But they generate theological understanding as well as receive it.

Currently there is a 'dumbing down' of all kinds of culture, not least in the media, and disastrously this is also prevalent in the church. Many people are giving up on the discipline of 'thinking biblically', partly because entertainment is replacing engagement with society. This is not what Mouw means by 'people's theology'. Rather, he means that theology is a community act. It is done by all of the people all of the time. If the theologians do not talk to the people, they talk only to other theologians. If the people are not willing to grow into theological maturity, then the church will be stunted in its growth and ineffectual in the world. Theology can be made only in community.

At this point we return to the problems of the attractiveness of magic in a technological society. We Christians want to fuse the reality of life today with our rich and long theological tradition in order to be able to speak to the concrete problems affecting the lives of ordinary people. Yet we must do so without succumbing to magic (so close to spirituality) and without adapting the life of prayer to an exercise in problem-solving. In short, we must avoid anything that would force God to do our will because of the pressures on us to demonstrate his efficacy and relevance.

The Christian mind

It is the search for a way of dealing with this 'middle ground' that has led to the development, over the last forty years, of the idea of the 'Christian mind'. This approach links theology and contemporary life – not only personal issues, but politics, economics, gender, technology, race and indeed all those issues with which we are struggling in our culture. The idea combines contemporary relevance with biblical authority. Although a great deal has already been written on this theme, the approach is in many ways still in its infancy.

Our discussion of politics, in chapter 2, sought a Christian approach to a set of issues that lie at the heart of contemporary debate on politics. This approach attempts to work out Christian principles in practical, political applications in legislation and local-council deliberations. The principles and the practice are linked by what I want to call 'the ladder of abstraction'. As we climb the ladder, we become closer to biblical theology. Even though there is still room for hermeneutical disagreement, we are discussing issues such as God's just nature or the inclusiveness of his kingdom. Yet at this level we are far removed from the drafting of Parliamentary Bills or the MP's surgery. At the other end of the ladder we find all kinds of people working on, say, one item of legislation. All of them, Christians and otherwise, have that wisdom that comes from being made in the image of God, and all must therefore listen to one another as they try to shape society. There may be little or no theological content to the resulting legislation. The intention of the Christian MPs involved in this process is that when enacted it might make our society more pleasing to God by curbing crime, improving education or healthcare, or whatever the topic was. In this case, the middle ground is that place where Christian MPs can bring together their Christian vision and pragmatic action and allow them to interact with each other. Of course, this may be done by personal prayer, but it may also be done by forming specific points of reference to guide them through the middle ground. For instance, their reading of the Bible may lead them to believe that God has a bias towards the poor, which they should reflect in their voting patterns; or to emphasize personal responsibility, and thus to be cautious about the growth of the welfare state. These reference points link biblical reflection with practical action.

In some cases the reference points are determined not so much by personal reflection as by Christian tradition. For instance, the criteria for assessing whether a war is just or not have been in place for hundreds of years, and must be taken into account by anyone grappling with those issues. Similarly, there has been a great deal of Christian thinking about issues of life and death, such as abortion or euthanasia, which can help us as a society to link biblical perspectives to our own personal or societal decision-making.

All this still leaves us without the element of certainty that people long for when they have to make decisions. (A man who wants guidance as to whom to marry might, in the face of such uncertainty, look at his horoscope, let his Bible fall open randomly, seek specific instruction from God, or read signs into everything he sees around him.) Even when we have made links between our theology and our situation, we still have to take personal responsibility for what we do. The fact is that the development of a people's theology requires us to fuse theology as doctrine with theology as story. People develop their theology as they live their lives. It is an evolutionary process, and may not follow a linear pattern but may change as they reach different stages in their life. Men typically follow a pattern in the shape of an upside-down 'U'. In early life there is a period of rapid ascension, when they are asking, 'What am I going to do with my life?' Then comes a plateau when momentum lessens during the mid-life period. Here they are asking, 'What am I doing with my life?' Lastly, in the period of descent, men ask, 'What have I done with my life?' This pattern is very important for an understanding of male spirituality. In telling the story of their lives, men at different stages express their spirituality differently because their needs are different.

The idea of pilgrimage expresses this movement of faith in Christ over our whole lives. It reminds us that developing a Christian mind is not an attachment to a set of concepts. It is organic. This applied teaching has to 'take root' in our lives.

God's story, our story

Human beings have always told one another stories, many of which draw on the great themes of life, death, courage, betrayal, sacrifice and love among others. We are surrounded by story. Recently, there has been a renewal of interest in Christianity as a story, not only because linear analysis may not reach somebody whose attention span is about three minutes, but because Christianity *is* story. The characterization of Christianity as narrative theology rather than as systematic theology does not reject the latter as an expression of eternal truth, or even challenge its relevance. The problem is not in the systematic theology. In fact analytical approaches to theology are not a problem at all. It is simply that they are not accessible to many people in a postmodern world, though they are still extremely important wherever they are appropriate forms of communication. But in a world where the soap opera is more powerful than the documentary, or where the documentary has to be presented in the form of a story so that people don't switch off, Christians also have the option of telling the gospel as story without departing in any way from its roots. Stories are powerful, as Jesus showed with his parables and allegories, because they capture the imagination whatever the listener's intellectual prowess.

Whatever the culture we live in, some things will never die. One of them is story. Not only has it existed since the very beginnings of human communication, but it is built into the universe; it is a part of God's transcendence. Stories weave purpose, meaning and information into the world. The history of the world is God's story, and the Bible is the record of that story. It is told with the authority of the one who knows the beginning, the middle and the end. To be a Christian is to say of the Bible, 'This story is my story.'

History is the story of every person's life. History from a biblical perspective has four great phases: creation, fall, redemption and consummation are the turning-points of the story told from Genesis to Revelation. But these are also the four great building-blocks of *my* story. I am created by God; I am fallen and sinful; I am redeemed by Christ; I am hoping for a new world. This story is my story. I own it. I am helping to make it happen, even in writing this book. This is part of my contribution to biblical history.

The Bible is also a story that invites my response as a reader. It invites me to act, and my action was part of God's intention when he caused it to be written. In their book *Truth Is Stranger Than It Used To Be*, Richard Middleton and Brian Walsh talk of Bible stories, such as the appalling rape of Tamar, in which Israel's response is inadequate. But what is *our* response to this story of rape and brutality? Such stories cry out for resolution, and this happens when anger is awakened in me on Tamar's behalf and I feel a passion for justice in situations outside the biblical text. The Bible has inspired action on my part by drawing me in and making my response part of the resolution of the tension in the story. Walsh and Middleton comment, 'This is entirely consistent with the Christian confession that the Bible is not a self-enclosed book of theoretical ideas but a covenantal text, which calls for our response to the God revealed therein.'[7] I thus become part of the drama by responding to the Scriptures, and my actions, based on this response, become part of the human race's playing out of the biblical drama. It is this 'covenant' between God's word and our response to it that forms the Christian tradition. We can respond appropriately only if we are soaked in the biblical story. The point is not just to repeat passages of Scripture that record an earlier generation's response to God. We can see how our ancestors in the faith responded to God in diverse contexts. We face a different context, and our lives do not have a script. Instead, we have been given the Holy Spirit to help us to be a faithful church in our generation.

Walsh and Middleton comment:

> ... if our praxis is to be faithful to the story, this requires taking the risk of improvisation that is creative, innovative and flexible. It is important that our performance not simply repeat verbatim earlier passages from the Biblical script. That would not be faithfulness for the simple reason that these earlier passages are not a script intended for our performance in a postmodern world but are the record or transcript of past performances of God's people. While we can see how our ancestors in the faith responded to God with varying degrees of faithfulness in a variety of circumstances, much of our difficulty in living as Christians today is that the concrete shape of our lives in the world is quite literally unscripted.
>
> Of course we know that we are to practice justice and economic stewardship, even in a society of power grabs and unlimited consumption. The trouble is how we are to embody these admirable goals is not specified. The Bible is neither strictly a script for us to enact nor a rulebook or repository of timeless truths into which we can dip when we need guidance. Whereas a script would prescribe exactly what we should do or say, leaving us very little and timeless truths would be too general and abstract to be of any real help in the day to day business of living.'[8]

These words illustrate the tension between tradition and change which we have encountered throughout this book. Our culture cuts the future loose from the past. It claims that we should look to our technological future, and live in the eternal present; but we do not need to deal with the past. Some, by contrast, would live in the past because it is tried and tested. They point to its wisdom, but also seem fated to replicate its errors and to be confused about the challenges of contemporary life. But tradition is a depository of truth from which we learn but which we do not have to replicate. We have a responsibility to relate to our own age appropriately, and can be creative in the way we do so. We bring together the need to understand the Bible thoroughly and the context in which we are living. In fusing them to form a people's theology, we can declare that both biblical history and our personal pilgrimage are 'my story'.

Facing two ways

The process of what John Stott has called 'double listening' both to God and to society[9] is a vital task for a healthy church as it recognizes its obligations to God and to humanity. For the church always faces in two directions. As Jürgen Moltmann has commented:

> The church will always have to present itself both in the forum of God and in the forum of the world. For it stands for God to the world, and it stands for the world before God. It confronts the world in critical liberty and is bound to give it the authentic revelation of the new life. At the same time it stands before God in fellowship and solidarity with all men and is bound to send up to him out of the depths the common cry for life and liberty.[10]

Whatever the age and whatever the culture, this mandate remains the same. Throughout this book we have noted the fourfold calling of the church: to be responsible for the world, to celebrate the world, to prophesy to the world and to suffer with the world. In all of these, the church stands facing both God and humankind. All four elements are present within the church's mission, for they are all essential if we are faithfully to reveal to the world what God has revealed in Christ.

So we take responsibility for God's world as trustees of it, attempting to maintain healthy communities, families and a just society. We call our society to celebrate that which is good and beautiful. We are prophetic in resisting all that is not of God, whether outside or inside the church. We act in solidarity with those who suffer, and feel their pain. To do all this is to be 'salt and light' in the world, not only resisting evil but also creating good. There is no perfect way of accomplishing these tasks. There are no new techniques to make those who resist the gospel accept it. It is by being Christ-like that the church most fulfils its commission. The church goes out into the world to evangelize, but what kind of church is it? To what extent does it carry with it the mark of Christ? It is the power of Christ rather than the power of technique that wins the world. Of course, everything the church does can be regarded as technique. The mode of worship, the method of preaching, the strategy of mission, could all be described as the deliberate application of technique to the church's calling. But if it *is* technique, we are in dire straits. Technique aims at achieving measurable success. But the message of the cross is sheer foolishness.

We must exercise our fourfold calling with a double emphasis on the person of Jesus. We must go, *as if* we were Jesus, because we are truly his representatives. We must also treat others with the respect and love that we would reserve *for* Jesus. They must not only see Jesus in us; they must feel what it must be like to be in relationship with Jesus.

This emphasis on relationship accords well with all that has been said in this book. One of its dominant themes has been the need for a re-examination of relationship and community within our society. As Dietrich Bonhoeffer once said, 'it is not Christian men who shape the world with their ideas, but it is Christ who shapes men in conformity with Himself'.[11] Not only do we offer the world a relationship with God; relationship is itself the method by which we offer it. Anything that detracts from that will blunt the church's mission. It is essential to recognize evangelism as the force that most changes the hearts of men and women. The gospel has always been reviled because Christians declare that it has been revealed from heaven and therefore carries the authority of God. In a postmodern world, this flouts the notion that all beliefs must be accorded an equal tolerance since truth cannot exist beyond language. Yet Christianity has persisted with this claim while watching cultures and philosophies come and go. In continuing the task of mission, the church cannot succumb to a postmodern view of truth, though it can learn a new openness from the postmodern mindset. It will continue to claim that the gospel is 'true truth', when postmodernity is a footnote in the history of human thought.

In recent years, statistics showing the extent of church decline have caused something of a panic in the church. The search for a new church culture has become intense. Many have suggested an 'answer' to the problems facing us. But there is no single answer, because there is no single question. Such an approach assumes that church culture is in some fundamental sense homogeneous. Of course, the Christian church is dedicated to living out the gospel of Christ. In that sense all Christians share the same message: 'one Lord, one faith, one baptism'. But there have always been different expressions of that faith, some of which originated in doctrinal disagreement, while others are stylistic. Sadly, some result from the empire-building of church leaders who have founded churches on the shifting sands of their own egos.

The evangelical wing of the church has seen the least decline over the last few decades, and many evangelical churches are well attended. The evangelical belief that the Bible has divine authority and that, handled rightly, its message is clear, simple and relevant to contemporary life, is a powerful one. Churches that proclaim it provide important educational models of how to teach and preach in an essentially modernist setting. While these models are based on principles of reason, these churches regard reason as a gift of God, serving the purposes of God, and would deny charges of rationalism.

Nevertheless, the danger that modernity may have infiltrated evangelicalism makes the task of 'making the invisible visible', discussed earlier in this book, even more pressing. In an article on 'Modernity and evangelicals', John Seel commented:

> ... the uncritical acceptance of modernity within evangelicalism ... is a serious matter, for modernity does not lead first to heresy, but to idolatry. Modernity's potent rewards will

come to replace our need for God. Our measures of success will be limited to the five senses and the most religious evangelical will be little different from a practical atheist. Like the Pharisees, we will be in error not because we do not know the scriptures, but because we no longer rely on the power of God.[12]

We could make the mistake of seeing the church's success as measurable in empirical terms, and find our mood swinging with the statistics of church growth. Alternatively, we could assess its impact in terms of power: for instance, its influence on public policy. Success could be financial, with the generous giving of churchgoers facilitating all kinds of innovative projects, church renovations and missions. It could be communal, taking community projects, concern for the poor and needy, and support for the local neighbourhood as evidence of social concern. It could be doctrinal, with the return of the church to its biblical tradition and the collapse of liberal theology. All these factors in assessing the church's success are excellent, but secondary. The church is called to be faithful. There is no measure of that. As Seel points out, we must be careful that apparent success does not come at too high a cost.

One development over the last forty years has been the appearance of 'brands' in the church. These brands overlap denominations. Even within evangelicalism there are five main ones: the conservatives, the charismatics, the radicals, the contemplatives and the post-evangelicals (though the latter would not place themselves in the evangelical camp). The conservatives focus on the Bible and on evangelism; the charismatics on the experience of the Holy Spirit; the radicals on liberation for the oppressed; and the contemplatives on waiting on God. The post-evangelicals are asking potent questions about the relevance of the others to contemporary culture. For good or ill, they are change-agents. They represent the most recent attempt to change the paradigm within which we live out the gospel, arguing that the world has changed so fundamentally that people can no longer hear what we are saying.

How should we regard this branding of the faith? One response would be to urge that we need one another. These Christian sub-cultures tend to have their own Christian festivals, favourite authors and preferred forms of worship, and it is all too easy to live cocooned within our own sub-culture and to stereotype those whom we perceive to be 'different' from us. It could be argued that Christian leaders need to show a willingness to break up these stereotypes, engage in conversation with the other 'brands', introduce new elements into church life and demonstrate that we need one another. This would be bound to strengthen the church as a whole.

The alternative response could not be more different. It would claim that people prefer to be with others who have something in common with themselves. Just as young men may meet to play football, and young executives for dinner parties, the existence of 'niche churches' offers people the opportunity to enjoy their preferred style of worship and fellowship among others with whom they are comfortable. On the face of it, there are many objections to this. Isn't the church supposed to demonstrate unity in diversity? How can a homogeneous group be a church? The defence is that these are unchurched people who would never come to any other church. Perhaps later they will join a church with a broader membership, but for now this is church for them.

We live in what some commentators have called 'the tailor-made society'. People no longer want to choose from a range of goods, but want goods that are tailor-made for them. People attend groups with others who are like-minded, but are quick to move on if they hit a problem. In recognizing this demand for tailor-made churches, the church encounters a familiar tension between authority and relevance. How far is the church willing to go in accommodating itself to contemporary culture in order to be relevant to it? Will it lose its authority if it does so?

As we try to formulate a way of being the church, we know that there are certain fundamentals without which we cannot be the church. But we must allow a great deal of latitude in the ways these fundamentals are expressed. There is no point in telling 'brand' churches to merge in order to express more fully the body of Christ. Open partnership would be a better way forward.

There are significant differences between 'brand' churches and 'niche' churches. Brand churches have broad-based congregations but a fairly narrow way of expressing the faith. Niche churches, formed around common interests, are exercises in mission to people who are unchurched. In a typically post-evangelical way, they draw on any Christian tradition. Both illustrate the tension currently felt in the church between independence and interdependence. But both have as their goal the realization of the church as the body of Christ. 'We are all members of one body'[13] wrote Paul, and while there will always be stylistic differences in the church we need to make every effort to lower the barriers between Christians.

This is also important for the church's impact on the community. If we see the renewal of community life as a priority (and it is an essential calling of the church to do so), we need to be effective within the community. This requires co-operation between local churches. whether of different denominations or different brands. Sadly, some churches defend their 'patch' and refuse to co-operate with other churches. Local communities are often mystified when what they regard as the small print of salvation keeps good work from being done.

The importance of conversation

In all this it is essential to keep on talking and listening to one another, to God and to our culture. The word 'conversation' conveys the sense that we live not in a static society but in an organic and dynamic one. It also draws together the personal, relational and political themes in this book. Conversation is at the heart of relationship. For most of us, it is through conversation that we know others and are known by them. Conversation involves listening. Without listening it degenerates into rhetoric, and rhetoric assumes power over those addressed. Open conversation, by contrast, generates equality. It generates dignity, respect and love, healing relationships and building community.

Zygmunt Bauman, who has devoted a book to the subject of conversation, says this about the importance of conversations on the subject of religion:

> I particularly value conversations which are meetings on the borderline of what I understand and what I don't, with people who are different from myself. For most of history, what people have disagreed most about is religion, which was the

topic of a very large proportion of conversations in the western world until about two centuries ago. I like conversations which discover that people with apparently differing standpoints can reach a meeting of minds on some subjects, limited though they might be. Since religion still continues to dominate discussion in many parts of the world, bringing believers and unbelievers together in conversation seems urgent as well as interesting.[14]

Isolation damages us. Individualism deceives us. In a world where we are encouraged to change our identity with our clothes, personal commitment to one another is essential. We have already seen that in our culture personal identity changes very quickly as the culture changes, especially among young people. Not only are people asked, 'Who do you want to be today?' but they treat relationships like questions that need answering. A woman asks a man, 'Who do you want me to be today?' She can adapt to his wishes, as he can to hers. They are not committed to a fixed identity. But if communities are to function properly, the people who comprise them need to be constant from one day to the next. True conversation, which is going to lead somewhere, depends on rooted security.

As Christians, we know we are loved and respected because God has drawn us into a divine conversation, not just a one-way revelation. As we consider how to renew the church's mission, we should not forget both the simplicity and the potency of conversation. It seems to me that there is a great deal of openness to conversation, in which Christians ought to be involved. Zygmunt Bauman offers an invitation to join in what he calls the 'new conversation':

> What is missing from the world is a sense of direction, because we are overwhelmed by the conflicts that surround us, as though we are marching through a jungle which never ends. I should like some of us to start conversations to dispel that darkness, using them to create equality, to give ourselves courage, to open ourselves to strangers, and most practically, to remake our working world, so that we are no longer isolated by jargon or our professional boredom.[15]

Earlier in this book we looked at the dogmatism, scepticism and cynicism that characterized the pre-modern, modern and post-modern societies respectively. None of these qualities can be a basis for conversation. Yet dogmatism is sometimes the attitude of Christians who speak to others about the faith. It is apparent in the way we explain the truth of the gospel to them: we have the truth and they do not; they have everything to learn and we do not. We ask them to bare their souls while we remain unwilling to make ourselves vulnerable. This one-way communication is more like public relations than Christian witness. But evangelism is not just passing on information about God that they need to know. We are also offering them the same invitation that was offered to us. We are all called to respond to that invitation by faith, and by a personal commitment to the one who has called us. It is important in our society to tell our story from the perspective of God's grace towards us, lest we portray ourselves as moralists who are Christians by our own merit. We cannot offer people dogma because we cannot offer them certainty. As Lesslie Newbigin has said,

> Our commitment is an act of personal faith. There is no possibility of the kind of indubitable certainty that Descartes claimed and that has been the criterion (spoken or assumed) for reliable knowledge in modern society. There is no insurance against risk. We are invited to make a personal commitment to a personal Lord and to entrust our lives to his service. We are promised that as we so commit ourselves we shall be led step-by-step into a fuller understanding of the truth.[16]

A story of hope

The fact that our story is unfinished does not mean that the end is not known. We are not postmodern vagabonds, as Bauman puts it, picking up scraps from the bins as we wander aimlessly through life. We are not tourists trying to make a biography by cutting experiences out of their context and pasting them into the album of the self, always moving on but never responsible. We are pilgrims, journeying towards a new world.

We are part of a story to which meaning is given by the actions of another. The defining moment of this story is Christ's resurrection. Because of it we know the end of the story. It is the resurrection that makes us into pilgrims; it teaches us that death is not defeat, that Jesus is the Christ and that God's promises will be kept. It puts the seal on seeing life from God's perspective and on saying, 'This story is my story.'

Christ's resurrection allows us to live in the light of the future. Indeed, we have to do so. We are dissatisfied with the present, not just with what the world has to offer but also with the aspects of our lives that are closest to us, such as our faith, our church, our friendships and our marriages. Wonderful as they may be, they are never ultimately satisfying. We are still filled with longing. Hope transforms the present by allowing us to live with our restlessness: the personal restlessness in each of us, and the restlessness of our corporate experience of being the church. Benedictine theologian Ronald Rolheiser puts it like this:

> It is non-negotiable. If you are alive, you are restless, full of spirit. What you do with that spirit is your spiritual life ... We are pilgrims on earth, exiles journeying towards home. The world is passing away. We have God's word for it! Too much of our experience today militates against the fact that here in this life all symphonies remain unfinished.[17]

This restlessness is an essential part of pilgrimage. It liberates us to admit it when things are going wrong, simply because things do go wrong in the lives of Christians. God does not need public-relations officers, advertising perfection in this life (what might be called the *Stepford Wives* approach to mission).

Paul represents the restlessness of Christian longing when he writes:

> I want to know Christ and the power of his resurrection and the fellowship of sharing in his sufferings, becoming like him in his death, and so, somehow, to attain to the resurrection from the dead.

Not that I have already obtained all this, or have already been made perfect, but I press on to take hold of that for which Christ Jesus took hold of me. Brothers, I do not consider myself yet to have taken hold of it. But one thing I do: Forgetting what is behind and straining towards what is ahead, I press on towards the goal to win the prize for which God has called me heavenwards in Christ Jesus.[18]

We are restless because Christianity *is* authentic, not because it isn't. Just as the provisional nature of democracy is evident when placed alongside the kingdom of God, so our experience of life is always tinged with longing. We protest, argue, desire and experiment because we are always looking forward.

Why is this important? As we try to work out our response to the Bible's message in our own culture, our listeners are asking fundamental questions about the ability of Christianity to be honest with itself and with them. This is a different kind of doubt. Formerly we talked about the relationship between doubt and truth. Here the question asked is about doubt and Christian experience. If it is true that our experience of the Christian faith is provisional because it is a pilgrimage, and if it is true that the Christian church suffers as much as it celebrates, how are these things expressed by Christians? Christians may know what they believe, but are they living it out? Many people are suspicious of the church and its message. We are claiming so much for the faith. Can they trust us? This is where love and respect come in.

Trust, respect and love

Amitai Etzioni saw the smallest unit of the community as being the family. Healthy family relationships will have a positive impact on the community. But within a Christian worldview our relationships are a response to the initiative taken by God. 'We love', John tells us, 'because he first loved us.'[19] We love because we are loved. We are not loved for a reason, otherwise the reason would be the condition of the love. We are loved because God loves us – unconditionally.

As we saw earlier, humanness is essentially about relationship based on a response to God. It is our relationship with God, not our family relationships, that is the primary relationship of trust. It is God who takes the initiative to renew and redeem the community. Everything else is a response to that love. So, having received, we give. We in turn take the initiative in love. Jesus characterized love in terms that have a direct impact on the life of the church:

> 'If you love those who love you, what credit is that to you? Even "sinners" love those who love them. And if you do good to those who are good to you, what credit is that to you? Even "sinners" do that. And if you lend to those from whom you expect repayment, what credit is that to you? Even "sinners" lend to "sinners", expecting to be repaid in full. But love your enemies, do good to them, and lend to them without expecting anything back. Then your reward with be great, and you will be sons of the Most High, because he is kind to the ungrateful and wicked. Be merciful, just as your Father is merciful.'[20]

As this passage clearly shows, reciprocity is not the basis of life in the kingdom. If we offer friendship only when it is offered to us, we do not need to draw on the power of God, or to resort to prayer, or to overcome fear. The love that took Christ to the cross is the love that creates relationship where there is none. It does so because of love. In doing so, it creates community where there was none. Christianity is a missionary religion because it is interested in creating community rather than just maintaining it. Love draws people in, irrespective of who they are or what they can give in return. This costly exercise of offering ourselves without our masks risks the pain of rejection in order to bring love to those who have never felt it. Such love crosses the social boundaries of society to create the diverse community called the church. The hallmark of its authenticity, as Jesus said, is love: 'By this all men will know that you are my disciples, if you love one another.'[21]

At the heart of that initiative is the security that comes from being loved just as we are. That in turn allows us the freedom to peel off the pretence we put up, both inside and outside the church, because we do not feel that we are acceptable as we are. This self-giving is the basis of trust. If I, as a Christian, hide behind a religious mask, in my dealings with non-Christians, there is no basis for trust. Only truth can be the basis for a relationship.

Since preaching is regarded with suspicion in a postmodern world, it is doubly important to live out our message. When others suspect us of trying to take power over them, it is most important that we serve them as Christ would do. Again, this can happen only if we are secure in who we are. Only the secure can serve.

Love must be based on respect, as we have already seen. Since God loves us unconditionally, we must do the same. When Christianity becomes institutionalized and insular, Christians become too used to associating only with other Christians. This not only perpetuates a sub-culture that can quickly become exclusive; it can also make Christians feel apprehensive about meeting people who are not Christians. The situation can become so artificial that it would be laughable if it were not so tragic. At its worst, Christians have few if any friends who are not Christians, or talk to non-Christians only when their church runs a special mission. Rather than sharing their life with friends, colleagues and neighbours, they have cut themselves off from them. Far from creating community, they are not even maintaining it. They are effectively rejecting the idea of creating community, and in refusing to pass on the love of God they are rejecting what it means to be the church.

Theologian Anthony Thiselton has said, 'The claims to truth put forward in Christian theology therefore call for love where there is conflict, for service where there are power interests, and for trust where there is suspicion.'[22] He uses the phrase 'non-manipulative love' to describe the unconditional character of Christian love. What the world is looking for is authentic Christlikeness. This is what stands between the fractured reality of postmodernity, with its despairing relativism, and the false certainty of a militant fundamentalism. Our calling is to have what Lesslie Newbigin has called a 'proper confidence' in what we believe.[23]

In his book *The Spirit of Life: A Universal Affirmation* Jürgen Moltmann comments:

> Because of the incarnation of God's love in the sending and self-surrender of Christ, the love of God is realized in love of our neighbor, and realized in such a way that the neighbor is

loved for himself, and not as a means to a higher end. 'If we love one another, God abides in us and his love is perfected in us ... he who does not love his brother, whom he has seen, how can he love God whom he has not seen?'[24]

Even when we are talking about justice in the political or social sphere, love should always be in our minds. Love and justice belong together, for they both express the heart of God. God has demonstrated both by bearing the marks of the cross. Nietzsche saw the influence of this God as oppressive. He could not have been more wrong.

Postscript

In this book I have attempted to recognize some of the major trends in our culture and reflect on their implications, both for our society as a whole and for Christian thought and action. How do we respond to these issues? After all, it is one thing to reflect, and quite another to live with integrity in such a society. Yet we are called as Christians to do even more than this. We are called to be a missionary church and to offer pastoral care in cultures where people's own understanding of who they are is changing all the time.

The new global perspective has become the context in which we work and live. One of the consequences this should bring is a cultural humility which those of us who live in the West need if we are offer something of worth to the rest of the world. Exposure to other cultures enriches our imagination and can show us new ways of living which we may not have dreamt of, even a few years ago. Despite our shoddy consumerism, multicultural Britain is much wealthier, culturally, than mono-cultural Britain ever was.

It is also vital for the church to see itself in a global perspective. So many of our debates, especially those which focus on institutional changes, are less important than global priorities. The western church has more to learn from the rest of the world than it currently has to offer, but we seem to lack the motivation to find out what is going on elsewhere, beyond the feedback from our own attempts at mission to other cultures. What can we learn from the church in Africa or India? The answer is: a great deal. Their theologians and church leaders have much to teach us if we are willing to listen. The burdens of church decline we are carrying seem even more oppressive when we try to lift them on our own. Our church missionary committees need to become listening and learning committees.

We are also living in a world in which human identity is under fire. The idea that we can choose to wear masks in different situations has been replaced by the belief that we have become those masks, so that the person has disappeared entirely; we have become so much a part of one another that the objective self is no longer necessary. The idea that this is the ultimate freedom is a dangerous distortion of the idea of freedom. The claim that God is dead led of course to the death of the soul; but now we are witnessing the death of the secular self. Gergen's idea that relationship precedes individuality is a parody of the biblical representation of people made in the image of the triune God. The notion that we have no fixed identities but are just a part of a socially constructed web of identities may lead to a renewed emphasis within Christianity on the God-given identity of the individual person. At present we are rightly emphasizing the fact that we are people in community, and that individualism has eroded community, which we need to recover. As society swings from one distortion to another, Christianity must bring different parts of the biblical revelation to bear on the situation.

This crisis of identity is exacerbated by the technological revolution we are currently going through. As we have seen, technology is ultimately about what we believe rather than what we can make. It views both the world and its people as resources to be used, and draws us away from wisdom to information. It is not about the hardware of which we are so enamoured, but about the power within it, which we do not control. It provides us with a way of life which has become essential to what it means to be human in the twenty-first century. In exploiting the earth, we have ourselves become exploited. We still worship at the altars of progress and efficiency, because we have no others left – even though we are aware that these gods are leading us astray. We are all potential resources for the triumph of future technologies, whether benevolent or not.

There is no nostalgic past to return to, since there is no going back to Eden. We must therefore learn to transcend the demands of technology. For Christians, the insight that this world is *for* something because it has been created by a transcendent God is the defining insight, which can provide hope for our future together. Worshipping that God and becoming a worshipping community in the world provides us with both the alternative vision and the motivation to live a different life. Christians, who live within a tradition of wisdom, are that alternative community. As technology undermines our society at a time when society has lost its confidence in its essential humanity, Christians have a responsibility to witness to the creator, who is the only source of transcendence.

The modern world is currently struggling with the disintegration of the structures and institutions that have always been the means by which we have expressed community. Whether the issue is marriage and family life, the legitimate authority of the nation-state or the nature of community, all is changing because of the tensions endemic in modern and postmodern cultures. Our society is marked by the erosion of tradition by the upsurge of choice, the consolation offered by consumption in a world where meaning has been questioned, and the suspicion that truth claims are bids for power. In this new world, human relationships have both benefited from and suffered under the renewed emphasis on human rights. Relationships between men and women have benefited from gender equality, but now need to pay attention to the balancing of responsibilities if family life is not to suffer even further than it has done already. Our relationships are under stress from our determination to have a high standard of living, even though we know that the quality of those relationships is suffering as a result.

Something has got to give. Perhaps we will see an age when both men and women work fewer hours because they are willing to have a lower standard of living in order to care more for their children and their elderly relatives. At present it is difficult to see how the unhappy trend towards increased isolation in our society will be reversed.

The community itself is also disintegrating. Ironically, the enormous amount of information that we now have about the wider world is delivered by means that most contributes to our isolation: the screen. Gazing at our televisions and computer screens makes us feel we are engaging with a wider world even while we are taking time away from relationships. Even when we speak with others, we have a tendency to regard it as networking, a technological concept that increases our tendency to see people as resources. The numerous contacts we get through the internet may widen our world, but may also lead to the 'saturated self' and to a tendency to spread ourselves too thinly rather than commit ourselves to rewarding relationships deep enough to be described as 'loving'. We still need personal involvement in community if it is to be healthy. The 'little troops' of the local neighbourhood, the Scouts, the Parent–teacher Association and so forth, are all necessary to sustain us as social people.

Globalization is changing the relationship of the nation-state to the rest of the world. Though there will always be a role for the state, we are increasingly aware that many of the decisions that affect our lives are commercial, and that those commercial interests are dominated by the multinationals. The closure of local branches of banks, and the sourcing of goods in the Third World instead of within our economy, are examples of decisions that have a huge impact on local communities but which are made for economic reasons in the boardrooms of multinationals. There is a danger that commercial interests will compete for the lowest labour costs in the world.

As we consider the changes happening in our own culture, we need to remember that we live in a world in which poverty is endemic. A quarter of the world's population lives on 65 pence each or less a day and less than 0.5% of world exports go to the least developed countries. There is much talk about global democracy and liberalism, but powerful countries are increasingly excluding countries in the South from decision-making. On the currency markets $1.5 trillion changes hands every day – the value of the world's total output is exchanged every four-and-a-half days. As talk of globalization becomes more prevalent, we need to remember the stark contrast between these statistics and the accompanying inequality in lifestyles that they represent. As the banks make hundreds of millions of dollars in profit for their shareholders, we must remember the poor.

This is the world in which the church makes its claim to represent the kingdom of God. It sees those outside the church as searching for something which the church has to offer. If this analysis is correct, the church has only to offer the right thing for people to be drawn to it. But in a postmodern world the issue is deeper than that. Many people do not know that they are meant to be searching. The church could go up to them and give of its best and they would not respond. One reason for this is the displacement of spirituality by consumerism, which temporarily satisfies the hunger for ultimate meaning. It some cases it is only when tragedy breaks into people's lives that they begin to find such a life shallow, and to search for other ways of living. Death in the family, illness or redundancy can, of course, turn people against God, but they can also turn people to him. Other people have many questions to which they do not feel the church is willing to listen. The church gives answers and preaches sermons but allows no space for questions, especially when they are ill-formed or arise from anger or disillusionment. Many of those churches that *are* attracting people are doing so because they combine an emphasis on loving relationships with space for people to ask questions, discuss issues and challenge speakers as well as to receive teaching. The Alpha course, which is now popular throughout the world, is a good example of this.

In our postmodern world we are thrown back on the nature of the gospel itself. People want to be told about the love of God, but they also want to feel the love of God. They do not want to hear preachers claiming authority; they want to recognize integrity in people from whom they can learn. They do not want to be taught by the apparently faultless; they want the encouragement of knowing that leaders are also vulnerable. They do not want to be given answers before they have had chance to ask questions. They do want not distance but friendship; not theory but practice; not analysis but story; not complexity but clarity. These are some of the preferences of the postmodern generation. They require a shift in the church's thinking away from church growth to church health. It is not the number of people in the church that counts, but the quality and integrity of its life.

Of course, postmodernity can be a threat to Christian witness. It will seem so to those who are not willing to consider how our culture is changing. It is damaged and confused, but other ages too have had their destructive episodes. Under the surface of our culture there is a hunger that can be met only by a Christianity that is Christ-like. Despite the challenges it brings and the unfamiliar landscape it creates, postmodernity may turn out to be the greatest opportunity the church has had in a long time to live out the gospel before the eyes of a watching world.

Notes

Introduction: Living with the presence of the future

[1] Graham H. May, *The Future is Ours: Foreseeing, Managing and Creating the Future*. (London: Adamantine Press, 1996), p. 6.

[2] These 'four voices of the church' developed out of a reading of Oliver O'Donovan's discussion of the church in his book *The Desire of the Nations* (Cambridge: Cambridge University Press, 1996), pp. 174–192. In his discussion of the church he talks of it as a gathered community, a suffering community, a glad community and a community that speaks the words of God. There are differences between the two lists but I am indebted to his own analysis.

1. Making culture visible

[1] Anthony Giddens, *Runaway World: How Globalisation is Shaping our Lives* (London: Profile Books, 1999), p. 22.

[2] Walter Brueggemann, *The Bible and Postmodern Imagination: Texts Under Negotiation* (London: SCM, 1993), pp. 2–3.

[3] Giddens, *Runaway World*, p. 21.

[4] Ibid., p. 27.

[5] Lesslie Newbigin, *Foolishness to the Greeks: The Gospel and Western Culture* (Geneva: World Council of Churches, 1986), p. 43.

[6] David J. Bosch, *Believing in the Future: Towards a Missiology of Western Culture* (Valley Forge: Trinity Press International, 1995), p. 23.

[7] From Clifford Longley's introduction to Jonathan Sacks, *Faith in the Future* (London: Darton, Longman and Todd, 1995), p. x.

[8] 'Let's do the Popomo a-go-go', *The Guardian*, 9 December 1995, p. 29.

2. Our shrinking world

[1] David Held et al. (eds.), *Global Transformations: Politics, Economics and Culture* (Cambridge: Polity Press, 1999), p. 2.
[2] Martin Jacques, 'The age of Asia: learning from the sunrise societies', *Demos Quarterly* 6 (1995), p. 6.
[3] Ibid.
[4] www.seatle99.org.
[5] John Micklethwaite, *A Future Perfect* (London: Heinemann, 2000), p. xx.
[6] Paul Hirst and Graham Thompson, *Globalization in Question: The International Economy and the Possibility of Governance* (Cambridge: Polity Press, 2nd ed., 1999), p. 20.
[7] Held et al. (eds.), *Global Transformations*, p. 445.
[8] Ibid., p. 46.
[9] Peter Melchett, 'Peer pressure: Lord Melchett talks to Roy McCloughry', *Third Way*, September 2000, pp. 16–19.
[10] Tom Bentley et al., *Getting to Grips with Depoliticisation* (www.demos.co.uk).
[11] Broadcast on 15 October 2000. Transcript and other material on the *Panorama* website: www.bbc.co.uk/panorama.

3. Truth on trial

[1] Anthony Giddens, *Beyond Left and Right: The Future of Radical Politics* (Cambridge: Polity Press, 1994), p. 83.
[2] Source: Office of Population Censuses and Surveys, *The Health of Our Children* (London: HMSO, September 1995).
[3] Source: ICM Research. 1,427 adults interviewed on 11–12 March 1994.
[4] H. Roberts and Darshan Sachdev (eds.), *Young People's Social Attitudes: Having Their Say – The Views of 12–19-year-olds* (Ilford: Barnardos, 1996).
[5] Source: P. Brierley and V. Hiscock (eds.), *UK Christian Handbook 1994–95* (London: Christian Research Association, 1996).
[6] General Synod debate 5 July 1996.
[7] Grace Davies, *Religion In Britain Since 1945* (Oxford: Blackwell), 1994).
[8] Peter L. Berger, *The Heretical Imperative* (New York: Anchor Press, 1979).
[9] Judg. 21:25.
[10] *Time* magazine, 4 December 1995.
[11] Stephen Hunt, 'Going back to basics', *Third Way*, April 1999, pp. 21–23.
[12] John Macquarrie, *Jesus Christ in Modern Thought* (London: SCM, 1990), p.

186 Living in the presence of the future

253. Cited in Alister McGrath, *Evangelicalism and the Future of Christianity* (London: Hodder and Stoughton, 1993), p. 153.

[13] Jean-François Lyotard, *The Postmodern Condition: A Report on Knowledge* (Manchester: Manchester University Press, 1979; English ed. 1984*)*, p. xxiv.

[14] Walter Brueggeman, *The Bible and Postmodern Imagination: Texts Under Negotiation* (London: SCM, 1993), p. 9.

[15] Ibid., p. 8.

[16] David Bosch, *Believing in the Future: Towards a Missiology of Western Culture* (Valley Forge: Trinity Press International, 1995), p. 13.

[17] Lesslie Newbigin, *Proper Confidence: Faith, Doubt and Certainty in Christian Discipleship* (London: SPCK, 1995), p. 680.

[18] John 8:32.

[19] Luke 22:27.

[20] John Carroll, *Ego and Soul: The Modern West in Search of Meaning* (Sydney: HarperCollins, 1999), p. 125.

[21] Mark Stibbe, *O Brave New Church* (London: Darton, Longman and Todd, 1995), p. 6.

[22] Carroll, *Ego and Soul*, pp. 125–126.

[23] Susan Sontag, 'Piety without content', in her *Against Interpretation* (London: André Deutsch, 1987), p. 249.

[24] Zygmunt Bauman, *Postmodern Ethics* (Oxford: Blackwell, 1993), pp. 20–21.

4. Living with ourselves

[1] Kenneth Gergen's phrase in *The Saturated Self: Dilemmas of Identity in Contemporary Life* (New York: Basic Books, 1991).

[2] Anthony Giddens, *Modernity and Self-Identity: Self and Society in the Late Modern Age* (Oxford: Polity Press, 1991), p. 162.

[3] Lesslie Newbigin, *Foolishness to the Greeks: The Gospel and Western Culture* (Geneva: World Council of Churches, 1986), pp. 34–37.

[4] See Charles Taylor, *Sources of the Self: The Making of the Modern Identity* (Cambridge: Cambridge University Press, 1989).

[5] Victor Seidler, *The Moral Limits to Modernity* (London: Macmillan, 1991), p. 12.

[6] Colin Gunton, *The One, the Three and the Many* (Cambridge: Cambridge University Press, 1993), p. 90.

[7] Seidler, *The Moral Limits to Modernity*, p. 14.

[8] Gunton, *The One, the Three and the Many*, p. 174.

[9] Zygmunt Bauman, *Postmodern Ethics* (Oxford: Blackwell, 1993), p. 240.
[10] Ibid.
[11] Ibid., pp. 241–242.
[12] Gergen, *The Saturated Self*, p. 75.
[13] Ibid., p. 77.
[14] Ibid., p. 80.
[15] Ibid., p. 254.
[16] Andrew Greely, 'Tribal consciousness', *Social Research* 37 (1970), p. 206.
[17] Marina Baker, 'The witches of Eastbourne', *The Independent*, 10 March 2000, p. 7.
[18] Alice Walker, *The Color Purple* (London: The Women's Press, 1983), pp. 167–168.

5. Living in relationship

[1] Alistair McFadyen, *The Call to Personhood: A Christian Theory of the Individual in Social Relationships* (Cambridge: Cambridge University Press, 1990), p. 31.
[2] Anthony C. Thiselton, *Interpreting God and the Postmodern Self: On Meaning, Manipulation and Promise* (Edinburgh: T. and T. Clark, 1995), p. 50.
[3] Jürgen Moltmann, *The Spirit of Life: A Universal Affirmation* (London: SCM, 1992), p. 255.
[4] Jürgen Moltmann, *The Trinity and the Kingdom of God* (London: SCM, 1981), p. 199.
[5] Simone de Beauvoir, *The Second Sex* (New York: Alfred A. Knopf, 1953).
[6] Roy McCloughry, *Hearing Men's Voices: Men in Search of their Soul* (London: Hodder and Stoughton, 1999).
[7] Part-time jobs are often low paid and have poor working conditions with little security. They are often aimed at women. Recent developments in British government policy intend to change this by improving the flexibility of the labour market and improving standards for workers. In particular, part-time staff will not be treated as second-class workers but will accorded the same rights and benefits as full-time employees.
[8] Source: Office for National Statistics, *Social Focus on Families* (London: HMSO, 1997).
[9] Ibid.
[10] Roy McCloughry, *Men and Masculinity: From Power to Love* (London: Hodder and Stoughton, 1992), pp. 238–247. See also Arlie Hochschild, *The*

188 Living in the presence of the future

    Second Shift: Working Parents and the Revolution at Home (London: Piatkus, 1989).

[11] Broadcast on 24 January 2000. Information and transcript on http://news.bbc.co.uk/hi/english/events/panorama/newsid_613000/613615.stm.

[12] Commissioned by *Panorama* and carried out by economist Susan Harkness (University of Sussex).

[13] Gail Sheehy, *Understanding Men's Passages* (New York: Random House, 1998), p.18.

[14] Lionel Tiger, *The Decline of Males* (New York: Golden Books, 1999), p. 5.

[15] London: Profile Books, 1999.

[16] Ibid., p. 4.

[17] Although the number of marriages declined in Britain in 1998, the divorce statistics also fell to their lowest level since 1990. We should bear that in mind when considering Fukuyama's hypothesis.

[18] The Organization for Economic Co-operation and Development.

[19] Fukuyama, *The Great Disruption*, pp. 32–33.

[20] Ibid., p. 47.

[21] McCloughry, *Hearing Men's Voices*, chapter 4.

[22] Fukuyama, *The Great Disruption*, p. 57.

[23] I am grateful to Elaine Storkey for this figure.

[24] Carried out by Kathleen Kiernan of the London School of Economics and published in *Population Trends*, December, 1999.

[25] Economic and Social Research Council, October, 1999.

6. Living in a political community

[1] Helen Wilkinson and Geoff Mulgan, *Freedom's Children: Work, Relationships and Politics for 18–34 year-olds in Britain Today* (London: Demos, 1995), pp. 100–101.

[2] Ibid., p. 17.

[3] A familiar theme in Hayek's work, but see his *The Fatal Conceit* (London: Routledge, 1990).

[4] Jonathan Sacks, *Faith in the Future* (London: Darton, Longman and Todd, 1995), p. 55.

[5] Interview with the *Sunday Times* magazine. Quoted in Andrew Marr, *Ruling Britannia: The Failure and Future of British Democracy* (Harmondsworth: Penguin, 1995), p. 319.

[6] Perri 6, 'Governing by Cultures', *Demos Quarterly* 7 (1995), p. 4.

[7] Norman P. Barry, 'The market still adequate?', a response to Jonathan Sacks, *Morals and Markets* (London: Institute of Economic Affairs, 1998), p. 32.
[8] Samuel P. Huntington, *The Clash of Civilisations and the Remaking of World Order* (New York: Simon and Schuster, 1996), p. 98.
[9] Philip Richter and Leslie J. Francis, *Gone but Not Forgotten: Church Leaving and Returning* (London: Darton, Longman and Todd, 1998), p. 85.
[10] David Landes, *The Wealth and Poverty of Nations* (New York: Norton, 1998).
[11] Cf. e.g. Mic. 4:4.
[12] Sacks, *Morals and Markets*, p. 23.
[13] Ibid., p. 53.
[14] Samuel Brittan, 'Two cheers for self-interest', in his *Capitalism with a Human Face* (London: Fontana, 1996), p. 52.
[15] 2 Cor. 8:13–15.
[16] E.g. Ps. 73.
[17] John 12:8.
[18] John Stott, *Issues Facing Christians Today: New Perspectives on Social and Moral Dilemmas* (London: Marshall Pickering, 2nd ed., 1990), pp. 245–248.
[19] Roy McCloughry, *The Eye of the Needle* (Leicester: IVP, 1990).
[20] E. F. Schumacher, *Small is Beautiful* (London: Abacus, 1974), p. 34.
[21] Roy McCloughry (ed.), *Belief in Politics: People, Policies and Personal Faith* (London: Hodder and Stoughton, 1996), p. 50.
[22] Amitai Etzioni, *The Spirit of Community: The Reinvention of American Society* (New York: Simon and Schuster, 1993), p. 15.
[23] David Selbourne, *The Principle of Duty: An Essay on the Foundations of Civic Order* (London: Sinclair-Stevenson, 1994), p. 274.
[24] All Etzioni's words in this subsection are taken from 'Finding the right balance: Roy McCloughry talks to Professor Amitai Etzioni', *Third Way*, June 1997, pp. 14–17.
[25] Michael Ignatieff, *The Needs of Strangers* (London: Chatto, 1984), p. 16.
[26] McCloughry, *The Eye of the Needle*, p. 73.
[27] Richard Neuhaus, *The Naked Public Square: Religion and Democracy in America* (Grand Rapids: Eerdmans, 1984), pp. 116, 124–125.
[28] Cf. Exod. 33:16.
[29] Lev. 26:12; cf. Exod. 6:7.
[30] 1 Sam. 8:6–18.
[31] Oliver O'Donovan, *The Desire of Nations: Rediscovering the Roots of Political Theology* (Leicester: IVP, 1998); cf. chapter 2.
[32] Ibid., p. 46.

190 *Living in the presence of the future*

[33] Ibid., p. 49.
[34] Rev. 1:7.

7. The impact of technological change

[1] '*O*' magazine, March 1996.
[2] In this section I am indebted to Neil Postman's thinking, in his *Technopoly: The Surrender of Culture to Technology* (New York: Knopf, 1992).
[3] We are called to reflect on these even if we cannot predict which of them may well come about. If a technology is to be subject to an enforceable government licence, as in some medical technologies, stringent restrictions on its use may be imposed before it is licensed. The more pervasive and powerful the proposed technology is, the greater its impact on human life and on the Earth, and the greater its unintended consequences may be.
[4] Both late capitalism and communism ignored the impact of industrial production on the environment. Indeed, when I was studying economics in the early 1970s I was still being taught that the air is a free good. It was only in my postgraduate years that Partha Dasgupta and others began to develop environmental economics in a sophisticated and systemic way.
[5] Jean-François Lyotard, *The Postmodern Condition: A Report on Knowledge* (Manchester: Manchester University Press, 1979; English ed. 1984), p. 4.
[6] Mary Midgley, *Wisdom, Information and Wonder: What is Knowledge For?* (London: Routledge, 1991), p. 45.
[7] Ibid., p. 43.
[8] Postman, *Technopoly*, p. 76.
[9] Ibid., p. 78.
[10] James Gleick, *Faster: The Acceleration of Just About Everything* (London: Little Brown, 1999).
[11] Tim Berners-Lee with Mark Fischetti, *Weaving the Web: The Past, Present and Future of the World Wide Web by Its Inventor* (London: Orion Business Books; 1999), p. 106.
[12] Ibid., p. 110.
[13] Perhaps one of the most interesting developments on the Net is that of published codes of ethics. Eight hundred and fifty of these are collected at the site of the Centre for the Study of Ethics in the Professions at the Illinois Institute of Technology. Many professions have codes of ethics; at the Washburn School of Law in Georgia, Web ethics is recognized as an important issue. Some of the Bar Associations are also well on their way to

producing codes of ethics for the use of lawyers who are members of the Bar and who wish to use the Web for advertising or consultation. In many ways the problem is not about professional use of the Web, but about the unprofessional use of the Web which cannot be controlled by voluntary codes of practice.

[14] Ps. 111:10.

8. The Spirit working in us

[1] Exod. 31:1–11.
[2] Gen. 11:3–4.
[3] Jas. 5:16–18.
[4] Richard Holloway, 'Evangelicalism: an outsider's perspective', in R. T. France and Alister E. McGrath (eds.), *Evangelicals and Anglicans: Their Role and Influence in the Church Today* (London: SPCK, 1993), pp. 181–182.
[5] Richard Mouw, *Consulting the Faithful: What Christian Intellectuals Can Learn from Popular Religion* (Grand Rapids: Eerdmans, 1994), p. 16.
[6] Ibid., p. 28.
[7] Brian Walsh and Richard Middleton, *Truth Is Stranger Than It Used To Be* (London: SPCK, 1995), p. 181.
[8] Ibid., pp. 183–184.
[9] See the introduction to John Stott, *The Contemporary Christian* (Leicester: IVP, 1992).
[10] Jürgen Moltmann, *The Church in the Power of the Spirit* (London: SCM, 1977), p. 1.
[11] Dietrich Bonhoeffer, *Ethics* (London: SCM, 1955), p. 18.
[12] John Seel, 'Modernity and evangelicals: American evangelicalism as a global case study', in P. Sampson, V. Samuel and C. Sugden (eds.), *Faith and Modernity* (Oxford: Regnum Lynx, 1994), p. 296, referring to Mark 12:24.
[13] Eph. 4:25; cf. Rom. 12:5; 1 Cor. 12:27.
[14] Zygmunt Bauman, *Conversation* (London: Harvill, 1998), pp. 88–90.
[15] Ibid., p. 97.
[16] Lesslie Newbigin, *Proper Confidence: Faith, Doubt, and Certainty in Christian Discipleship* (London: SPCK, 1995), p. 66.
[17] Ronald Rolheiser, *Forgotten Among the Lilies: Learning to Live Beyond Our Obsessions* (London: Hodder and Stoughton, 1990), pp. 8, 13.
[18] Phil. 3:10–14.
[19] 1 John 4:19.

[20] Luke 6:32–36.
[21] John 13:35.
[22] See Anthony C. Thiselton, *Interpreting God and the Postmodern Self: On Meaning, Manipulation and Promise* (Edinburgh: T. and T. Clark, 1995).
[23] See Newbigin, *Proper Confidence*.
[24] Jürgen Moltmann, *The Spirit of Life: A Universal Affirmation* (London: SCM, 1992), p. 250, quoting 1 John 4:12, 20.